D0640541

MAUD'S HOUSE

Also by Sherry Roberts

Greensboro, A New American Metropolis

MAUD'S HOUSE

A Novel

Sherry Roberts

Papier-Mache Press
Watsonville CA

10 9 8 7 6 5 4 3 2 1

First Edition

ISBN: 0-918949-32-7 Hardcover

Cover art by Anna Price-Oneglia

Cover design by Cynthia Heier

Photograph by Julie Knight

Typesetting by Prism Photographics

Library of Congress Cataloging-in-Publication Data

Roberts, Sherry, 1954-
    Maud's house / Sherry Roberts. — 1st ed.
       p.   cm.
    ISBN 0-918949-32-7 (hardcover : acid free) : $18.00
      1. City and town life—Vermont—Fiction.   2. Women artists—
Vermont—Fiction. I. Title.
PS3568.024736M3   1994
813'.54—dc20   94-715
                                    CIP

To Tony,
who always believed I could make my writing sing,
even though I can't carry a tune.

MAUD'S HOUSE

Step Right Up and See Maud's House

Once this house was covered with tattoos.

Pictures of trees and monsters and animals trickled from my fingers like blood. They spread over the walls and the furniture and the dishes. Scenes slithered across the undulated siding. Portraits yawned on downspouts, like the mirror faces in a carnival fun house.

Before I was born, this place was nothing but an old Vermont farmhouse. Misshapen by generations of New Englanders, every one a frustrated architect. Rooms were added as families grew, as wives squirreled away money, as whims took the owners. There was no grand plan, just a grand passion for leaving a mark.

I grew up here. I have those people inside of me. I too have always needed to change my world. I could never be satisfied with just sitting on a porch step and leaving life alone. There was so much inside of me, so many lively, creative itches that demanded with the volume of a foghorn to be scratched. Once all I could feel was creation. It was my food, my water, my air.

I painted here. I made my mark on everything. My house wasn't just a house; it was a canvas, a roadside attraction. Once people went out of their way to see my house. They asked for directions in town. They asked Wynn Winchester the beautician or Frank Snowden at Snowden's General Store or the Reverend Samuel Swan as he raked the leaves in front of the church. Wynn, Frank, and the Reverend didn't mind.

"Head north on Highway 100," they said. "Two miles out of town hang a right on Beaver Creek Road. Probably won't be a sign; damn kids keep stealing it. Just look for the pole. It's a dirt road. Follow it, oh, three miles, and you'll come to Maud's house. Can't miss it. You'd have to be *blind* to miss it. The colors scream at you, like a rock 'n' roll band."

A van full of hippies, high on Canadian weed and an Expos win, found it. "Cool, man," they said, "psychedelic siding." So many people discovered my house, in fact, that Papa started a guest book, like the museums have, for people to sign. A record of who'd been here and what was on their minds at the time.

"Professors Skillington, Dillington, and Jones. Harvard. Interesting blend of the primitive, mystic, and totemic . . ." They spent three days with us, roaming the house, eating our food, taking notes, and shaking their heads. They found correlations between my painting and the works of the masters. I agreed with everything they said and would have gotten away with it, too, if I hadn't asked, during a long monologue by Professor Skillington on the place of the horse in abstract art, "Miró who?"

"Bill and Sally. Perryville, Missouri. The cutest little house we ever saw." They discovered the house by accident. "Oh, look at that house," Sally said, poking Bill in the ribs until he stopped. They came upon the house suddenly, and it startled them. They stared at it as if it were a deer caught in their headlights. They got out of the car, approached it with caution, then began snapping pictures.

"Sandra, Nick, and Jack. Berkeley. Thank you." I liked them. They arrived looking for something. They touched the house with gentleness, the way you caress the soft spot on a baby's head. They asked if they could camp in the yard for the night. "You can camp here forever," I said, totally enchanted by their free smiles and quiet acceptance. But they didn't. In the morning they headed down the road, their van with the peace sign painted on the side backfiring as they disappeared over the horizon.

It was a house that called to strangers and strange people. Like my husband George. But let's not talk about him now. George killed the house, before he died himself. George was such a stinker. He still is.

On my fourth birthday, my father gave me the house, home to the Calhouns for generations, the place where my father and grandfather were born. "Gave her every nail, board, and shingle," my father used to tell our tourists. Papa became rather possessive about the people who used to stop and admire my house; he felt a responsibility to "our tourists" and their sight-seeing pleasures. He never minded when they interrupted him milking a cow or repairing an ax handle. He had public relations in his blood. "Twelve rooms," he told them. "And Maud's painted every square inch."

While other parents made threats, swatted bottoms, took away television privileges, my father said: Go ahead. Go ahead and draw on the walls.

He had nothing against discipline.

He was not into pop psychology and the benefits of letting children express themselves.

My husband, George, said he was crazy.

I said, "No, he just loved me."

Psychologists say concert pianists, Olympic swimmers, great mathematicians, renowned surgeons, gifted sculptors don't succeed just because of their natural genius. They become what they become because they had mothers and fathers who provided pianos to bang, pools to swim in, toys to tinker with, frogs to dissect, clay to shape. I said, "Think of the house, George, as a frog."

George thought of it as real estate.

I knew I couldn't keep George out of this, so I might as well talk about him. I met George the day I buried my father. There I was, fresh from the funeral, wondering why everything seemed changed, banging my shins on the coffee table, when George knocked on the door. He was like all of our tourists, curious about the house. I burst into tears. That was my father's province. Public relations. The tourists.

"I don't understand," I sniffled. "All my life that coffee table has been in the same place." I rubbed my leg and looked at George in confusion. "You asked what? The house?"

George stepped inside the door, asked where the kitchen was, and took charge of my life. "You need two aspirin and an ice bag for that leg."

George's timing was perfect. I know now George and my father wouldn't have lasted a day in the same house. Papa didn't like Professors Skillington, Dillington, and Jones, either. He sang and danced when they left. And now George is gone, too, cracking up his car on a curve on Highway 100. Up in heaven, I bet Papa's feeding the jukebox.

Papa had been right about Professors Skillington, Dillington, and Jones; what they knew about true creation would fit on a postage stamp. Of course, I knew who Miró was. I'd read about him in a book about artists from the Round Corners Library. That's where I got my ideas at first—from books. When I painted the pictures in the dark, narrow, back stairs, I had to use a flashlight. I pretended I was a prehistoric woman in some cave in France, one of the first artists of all time, and the flashlight was flame.

A corner of the Sistine Chapel was my model for the bathroom ceiling. My father looked up as he shaved in the morning and saw men welcomed into heaven or sentenced to hell. "What a way to start the day," he growled.

We ate on plates, the undersides dripping with the images of melted watches. We slept under the sensual influence of Picasso bulls. Being a farmer, I thought my father would appreciate that touch of the bucolic. Night after night, he contemplated the furiously erotic creatures strutting about his ceiling, pumped up with power and hormones and nature. He said he thanked the Lord they couldn't get to his cows.

The whole house was a canvas. The pots and pans, the tables and chairs, the grocery bags, the flowerpots, the kitchen cabi-nets, the rocks in the yard, the buckets in the barn. Nothing was safe.

My father constantly complained/boasted to Milky Way, our pet cow. "Oughta see what she's done to the bathroom. I've had nightmares that looked better than that. Scared the shit out of me."

"Papa!"

He'd go on, pretending he didn't hear me, devoting his full attention to scratching the place behind Milky Way's ear. "Told her she oughta tone down the places where a man first sits in the morning."

I have always preferred a clear and simple style. I've never been one for flinging paint on a wall with a big bowie knife or scraping it around with an old automobile license plate. I like a cow to look like a cow.

Back then, when I used up paint faster than Snowden's General Store could stock it, or so it seemed, I worked mostly on the large side. I painted murals so big and true they were mistaken for real life. Once, while my father was visiting Aunt Marian in Buffalo, I painted a replica of the barn door on the side of the barn. In the painting, you could see Milky Way waiting for breakfast. The first day home from Aunt Marian's, Papa trudged out into the misty morning to do chores. "Hold your horses, Milky Way," he mumbled, rubbing his eyes, buttoning his jacket, plowing straight into the painting. Almost broke his nose.

Yes, once I was that good.

Good enough to put people's noses out of joint.

1

Granite Is 25,832 Times Harder Than the Human Toe

The problem is this: I talk to George more now than when he was alive.

Tell them, George.

Describe some of our long existential discussions. You can't remember the lyrics? Cute, George. Many people happen to think country-and-western songs are extremely existential. I don't know why I talk to you, when you don't even listen to country music.

I'm not sulking. I have never sulked in our entire married life, although I had plenty of cause.

Name one? How about the house, George?

That always shuts him up.

I remember the night George suggested we repaint the house. Our neighbor, T-Bone, who was over for dinner, choked on the asparagus. I can still hear T-Bone's gasp, more clearly than a marriage full of George's words. *"Mon Dieu,"* he said. (T-Bone always lapsed into the language of his French Canadian boyhood when upset.) It was the year George hoped to beat out Frank Snowden for town moderator. Although one didn't exactly campaign for town moderator, George apparently thought it wouldn't hurt to spruce up the place, to present a more organized image to the community.

"Paint the house?" I didn't understand. "What color?"

"White is nice," George said.

T-Bone's fork clattered against his plate, asparagus still speared by the tines.

The dinner table, I have found, can be a damned awkward

place, basically because people attempt communication there.
Married people have the worst inner clocks when it comes to
synchronizing conversation. When she is all abuzz, he is morose.
When he won't shut up, she is as talkative as the roast.

"Talk to me," he says.

"What do you want me to say?" she says.

"Anything," he says.

"Anything," she says.

Anything used to drive George crazy.

Like I said, now it's blah, blah, blah between George and me.
So many nights I fall asleep hugging a Rolling Rock, my jaws
tired from parleying with George. And when I wake, my mouth
is dry, making me wonder if I even talk to George in my sleep.

I have no professional explanation for these dialogues. My
friend Wynn Winchester, who is knowledgeable in most matters
of the mind, says I'm still angry with George. Not because he left
me, wrapped his car around a telephone pole, and had a secre-
tary that made a fool of herself at the funeral. No, it has to do
with the painting.

Wynn has an entire theory about what she calls my "George
Period." She counts off on her fingers: (1) My work got progres-
sively smaller in size while living with George; scenes that once
filled the side of a barn began to fit nicely on a postcard. (2) My
subject matter became increasingly nonhuman. (This is a refer-
ence to the cows.) (3) And why, she asks with the superiority of
Sherlock Holmes, didn't I ever paint the *things* George gave
me? Like the microwave and pasta-making machine, for in-
stance.

"No, Maud," Wynn shakes her head, "this whole blocked
artist business began way before George turned the fun house
into the White House. It began the day you let him into your
house." Not to mention my heart.

Wynn is so smart because, as the owner of a beauty salon, she
subscribes to several journals for the edification of her informa-
tion-hungry clientele and the enjoyment of coupon clippers.
Wynn doesn't put much faith in that quack publication, as she

calls it, the *New England Journal of Medicine;* she goes
straight to the real resource: *Cosmopolitan.* Wynn has time to
read those authoritative studies because business is slow until her
morning sickness subsides and she can face perming chemicals
with a settled stomach.

In my experience, reading is a dangerous thing in the wrong
hands. Take Odie Dorfmann, sheriff, town selectman, a politi-
cian with reelection on his mind and unkept campaign promises
on his conscience. In short, a dangerous person. Last election,
Odie guaranteed to bring more art to Round Corners. Odie read
in the *Burlington Free Press* about a town in the Midwest that
built an entire tourist trade around an old fresco in a church, and
he became obsessed with the idea of commissioning a work of
art for the Round Corners Town Hall. It had to be big and
powerful, something part King Kong and part Thomas Hart
Benton. And it had to be about Round Corners. That is where I
came in and how I ended up this crackling fall day, in a grave-
yard, ruining my favorite cowboy boots.

"Damn you to hell, George," I whispered, kicking George's
headstone with all my might. Wynn's magazines would diagnose
that I have a lot of displaced anger. There was nothing displaced
about it. George and Odie, the baseball buddies, refused to
believe me when I said I couldn't paint anymore. They thought I
was just being "difficult." They didn't believe that, over the years,
the spark had dried up and drifted away. The Georges and Odies
of the world get a picture of you in their heads and, like snapping
turtles, they never turn it loose. To them, I was, and always
would be, Maud the artist. I was artist before I was friend or wife
or lover.

I couldn't imagine George or Odie studying one of my paint-
ings, sighing with longing, and saying, as my father once did,
"Damn, that musta been fun to do." Neither one could distin-
guish between product and process. If you put in the time, you
made the dime in their world.

T-Bone knew there was no such thing as art on demand. He
was a farmer. He knew what it was like to work his spirit into the

land, to knead his soul into the soil, and to come up flat, empty-handed—stunted crops and stillborn calves. Too much sun, not enough. The right vitamins, the wrong feed. It didn't matter in the end, T-Bone the dairy farmer used to tell me. What mattered was to feel the sunshine on your cheek, to gaze down a row of corn so neat and straight it looked like aliens had made it with their high-tech spaceships, to rub your cold hand against the warm neck of a cow.

Since Odie believed my artistic impairment to be of a nonexistent nature (not to mention psychological, temporary, and easy to fix if I just stopped pampering myself and put my mind to it), he proceeded to hound me about the Round Corners masterpiece night and day. Cornering me in Snowden's General Store, he bent my ear with questions: When was I going to start? How long did I think it would take? And did I think I'd be using any real-life characters from Round Corners? Perhaps a lawman?

I gave George's headstone another whack; pain shot up my leg. I must have bought the hardest damn rock in Vermont. The granite deflected the toes of my western boots as if it were made of diamonds.

The grave is one year old. There is grass but it's sparse; you can still make out the mound of dirt under the leaves. The grave is about six feet long. Although I bet if you stood George up against one of those criminal catchers in the bank, the height markers on the doorjamb, he'd tick off at about five-ten. That's standing straight, which George always did. And that's with his blonde hair blow-dried to the correct fluff. When George went to the bank, or anywhere, his hair was styled, and he wore a crisp suit.

Those damn suits. I was picking up George's suits at the dry cleaner's even after he died. "That'll be eight dollars," the clerk said. Eight dollars, I fumed, wishing I'd never found the damn laundry receipt.

Eight bucks. I booted the headstone.

"That's not really going to help." I turned to the man leaning against the maple, one leg crossed over the other, his hands casually shoved into the pockets of his suit pants. He was frowning. T-Bone is practical to a fault, something to do with his French-Canadian farmer genes. And he is a true friend, another thing to do with genes, those passed down by some distant Canadian Mountie who married and had children when he wasn't tracking criminals in the snow.

The wind whipped around me, stirring up the dead autumn leaves, sending them into the air with a clatter. They grabbed at my legs and hair, like a mother's fingers trying to soothe a child in a tantrum.

The Round Corners Cemetery is as old as the invention of the shovel. It clutches a hillside north of town on land a goat would think twice about tackling. When we were children, Wynn and I used to pass the cemetery on the bus ride home from school. We argued: Were the dead really lying down or standing up? Were they clinging by their fingernails inside their coffins eternally fighting the force of gravity?

The Round Corners Cemetery climbs the hill and stretches into a neighboring cow pasture. Plenty of room for expansion. "For all it's needed," George used to say. Round Corners has only five hundred *living* people. An earthquake could wipe out the entire town, suck it into the center of the earth, and the cemetery would still have room to spare. Such burial zoning and planning baffled George the real estate agent. He looked at that cow pasture waiting for Round Corners's deceased and saw condos. The prospect of mansions among the mausoleums put a cold smile on the face of George the accountant.

Winter was as kind as George when it came to the cemetery. It wore at the headstones, each year shrinking them a little more, bone-colored slabs growing smaller and smaller, the way old people do. The tombstones were like Popsicles. The Vermont weather constantly sucked and licked at them. Some were nothing but nubs, and nearly impossible to read.

If you strained your eyes, you could make out Snowden, Smith, Elder, Pratt; they came first and farthest on ships across the ocean. Then the less worn and easier to read were

Desautels, LaBerge, Champlain, Soutiere, those who later rolled
down from the North like a snowball. The clearest were
Solomon, Goodsell, Martinez, Wysecki; they melted into the
Vermont pot, either drawn here by the beauty of the Green
Mountains or driven here by jobs they could no longer stand, by
cities that smothered them and drained their heart, by bumper-
to-bumper traffic and breathless crowds, by the fear that kept
them from dashing to the convenience store for a carton of milk
in the middle of the night.

And now, there was George, expanding the cemetery. You
could read his shiny new headstone a mile away.

Furious, I did a Mexican hat dance around George's grave,
kicking out at the granite.

It always disturbed T-Bone to see me like that—out of control,
letting George make me crazy, kicking dead people.

Tomorrow I would wake up full of guilt, not about George, but
about T-Bone. I would remember the sadness in his eyes and
hate myself. I always wanted to tell him: I'm not really like this,
please don't think less of me; it's just George. But he knew that.
T-Bone knew me better than I knew myself.

T-Bone was so gentle; he wouldn't last a minute in the real
world, a world where the most important things were not
milking cows and tap dancing. He was forty last birthday. I have
known him since he immigrated to Vermont from Canada with
his uncle André at the age of thirteen. I was eight. They bought
the farm next to ours. T-Bone took over at the age of nineteen
when a drunken cow fell on Uncle André and killed him. The
cow didn't get soused on purpose. It was in the wrong place at
the wrong time, hanging its head over a fence when some kids,
out to be wild and wondering about a cow's capacity for Rolling
Rock, happened upon it.

Some mornings I get up early, before the sun, and drive over
to T-Bone's. I watch him dance as he milks the cows. Something
about his body swaying, circling cows and milking machines, lifts
my spirits. The sound of the taps on the bottom of his L.L. Bean
boots clipping the concrete fills the barn with rhythm and steals

into my soul. I close my eyes . . . and it's as if I were painting again.

T-Bone interrupted the hat dance. "Have you had breakfast?" he asked. I shrugged. "You know you get testy when you haven't eaten. A nutritious breakfast is important. I should have brought the cinnamon rolls. I made them with raisins, your favorite." T-Bone nibbled on his bottom lip. "Yes, I should have brought the rolls."

T-Bone's a worrier. His mind runs a thousand "what if" scenarios a day, like a computer calculating contingency plans for the government. Nuclear holocaust, milk subsidies, tomorrow's forecast, anything is fodder for his overactive imagination. He worried when I was painting and when I stopped. He worried when I married George and when I buried him. He worries when no birds come to the feeder and when he can't keep it in sunflower seeds. He is a tall, lean, anxious man. He burns calories like autumn leaves; his insides—every organ, muscle, and ligament—must chug and churn twenty-four hours a day.

T-Bone stopped pacing, glared at me, growled something to the effect that I needed "something in that beautiful body besides beer," and resumed marching up and down the cemetery.

Unlike T-Bone, I don't exhaust my metabolism. I also don't smoke or chew my fingernails or crack my knuckles. I meditate and wait. I sit on the hard porch step of my house, my legs wrapped around me like a flowing robe, and study the faded painting of Milky Way on the side of the barn. I listen. I hear the busy chatter of the leaves, the voice of autumn, the whisper of my breath echoing through the passages of lungs and heart and time. Some days I hear T-Bone pacing over at his farm a mile away.

But the meditation stopped working. And the painting went wrong. I tried harder, and George tried harder. Our beer budget grew. George died. But the painting didn't come back. The beer budget doubled. Odie decided to turn Round Corners into the Louvre of Vermont (no telling what *that's* going to do to the beer budget). And I ended up in a graveyard on a cold October morning, a thirty-five-year-old artistic has-been acting like a two-year-old tantrum queen.

Some might say I put too much store in the inner self. Artists will. We're always reaching for the unseen mystery on the top shelf, our bodies stretched heavenward, ready to fly off the common chair of reality. So it can be disorienting when we feel too old to reach, can't even find the energy to drag the chair over to the shelf.

I learned how to meditate from a little man who called himself Raj. He had a huge self, yet hardly one at all. He liked Jackie Kennedy, spy thrillers, and my house. I was thirteen when Raj passed through on a whiff of Eastern mysticism.

My husband, George, wafted into my life on the last gasping fumes of an aging Volvo. "Could I use your phone?" he asked. "Sure," I said, and let him into my life. I don't want this to sound too romantic, like love at first sight. I prefer to think it was pure timing. Not that George couldn't be charming, occasionally. But there I was, nineteen and never before left to my own devices. We married fourteen days after we met, two weeks after I buried my father. I learned how to drink Rolling Rock beer while living with George. He liked Richard Nixon, baseball books, and taxes. George was an accountant and a real estate agent.

I watched T-Bone till the cemetery's leaves. He paced like a machine. Back and forth. Plowing a furrow through the leaves. I closed my eyes and listened. He was plowing his way to China. When I opened my eyes, I was surprised I could still see him. I expected there to be only his head sticking up from the excavation, floating above the hole bodiless, pacing back and forth like a duck at a carnival shooting gallery.

"It is especially important to eat at a time like this . . ." he said. I tuned out the rest of the lecture.

Across the cemetery, under a balsam fir, is my father's grave, next to the grave of my mother, who I never met. It is a pretty spot, not so steep that they have to cling to anything but each other. My father said they were the perfect couple. They could send each other's heart racing with just a smile. My mother looked like me, and my father called her his Wild Gypsy Rose. Her name was Rose. She never painted a picture. She did, however, draw caricatures to make my father laugh. He kept them in a shoe box in the closet. At night I'd hear him in his room, chuckling, and I'd know he had broken out the shoe box again. She died two days after I was born, asking for paper and pencil to draw "the scrunched-up face" of her daughter. The nurse promised the paper after she rested. My mother never awakened from her nap.

"Dance for me," I said to T-Bone.

"What?" That stopped him.

"Dance for me, T-Bone."

How many times have I said those words? I have loved his body for as long as I can remember. From the beginning, I have been fascinated by the way T-Bone's body flows. It is slender and neat and slides through space. He's at ease in the tug and pull, a part of moon and tide and gravity. That was something I knew nothing about; I was born a klutz. I envied his ease in the cosmos. He interested me, and so I spent half my childhood following him around. I studied him. I wanted to feel that motion. When I was twelve, I began to make sketches, which embarrassed him at first. Probably no teenage boy likes to be sketched. But T-Bone was especially shy. I've never known anyone so bashful. It took years, and constant nagging on my part, to get him to open up and talk to me.

I remember once when he was fifteen and I was ten. We were sitting on a bale of hay in the barn. The light streamed in over T-Bone's shoulder and cut through his profile like a chisel. He was telling me that his real name was Jacques Leon Thibeault and that Thibeault was a proud name in his home in the Laurentians.

"Why do you let them call you T-Bone then?" I asked.

T-Bone shrugged. "My uncle says kids will be kids. They will soon tire of it." But they never did and the name stuck like meat to the ribs.

"Well," I said, "I like it."

"You do?"

"Sure, it has personality. You wouldn't want to be any old Tom, Dick, or Harry. You're special."

That embarrassed him. But, I noticed, from that day on, he never had any trouble talking to me.

T-Bone was dressed for talking that morning in the cemetery. He had an appointment at the bank and was outfitted in a marvelous double-breasted suit that some Montreal tailor whipped up for him. The suit was cut and sewn for a man accustomed to the feel of leather briefcases, elevators, and clean, climate-controlled offices. It made T-Bone look long and polished and sure of himself.

He has always been a handsome man with thick, dark hair, blue eyes, and a smile that has a warm effect on everyone, even strangers. In the suit, he looked capable of flirting with a pretty woman or flipping a credit card at a clerk. I knew he didn't own a credit card and that, except for me, he was tongue-tied around most women. Women found him attractive, though. Like me, they loved his smile. It was a charismatic crinkling of facial muscles, something you'd expect on a Kennedy, totally wasted on a person as shy as T-Bone.

Tap-dancing T-Bone, everyone called him. Dance for me, I silently begged. Let me lose myself in you.

"Remember the time I asked you to pose in the nude?"

T-Bone blushed. "You were a precocious child, Maud."

"Even at the age of fourteen, I knew a good body when I saw one."

T-Bone muttered in French, shifted uneasily, and tugged at his silk tie. He glanced at the watch I gave him on his last birthday. It was one of those new Swiss ones, fine parts in a plastic case, incredibly light. He says he can't even feel it on his wrist. I wanted to buy the one with polka dots on the face and a purple and yellow checkered band. Or how about the one that smelled like bananas? He said the grey pin-striped would be fine.

I have never worn a watch. Until I met George, I was not aware of the passage of time, of years that escaped and hours that dragged. All the clocks I knew were on canvas and, for a while during my surreal period, drippy and melted. During my George period, clocks and everything else I painted became precise little things on a Maud Calhoun greeting card—sold winter, summer, spring, and fall at the cash register at the Round Corners Restaurant. In recent years, that has been my only art, greeting cards, with tiny pictures that couldn't possibly matter in the great scheme.

"So, how am I to do Odie's painting, George?" My boot hit the gravestone with a clunk. "This is all your fault. I should have shot you before you had a chance to leave me. Saved the car."

T-Bone sighed. "George couldn't help it that Odie Dorfmann was his best friend."

"Don't defend him. He knew Odie was running for reelection on a cultural platform. To nail the arts vote, Odie said. George encouraged him. He thought they could build it up into a tourist attraction, give the local economy a shot in the arm. 'Fine,' I told George and Odie, 'just don't involve me.' 'But Maud,' George said, 'you're the one with experience in tourist attractions.'"

"It was bad luck that Odie won the election," T-Bone said.

"He was running unopposed."

Sure things. George liked sure things, situations he could control. He was good at that sort of thing, organizing the world, taking action, solving problems, putting things right. I've often thought George would have done wonders in the Middle East. He believed in new beginnings. If one idea didn't work, he tried another. He refused to let himself get bogged down by historical baggage, negative attitudes, insecurities. Those were children of the past, and George was a child of the present.

When I first married George, I desperately needed someone with that quality. I have never been any good at taking care of myself—logistically. I could have a headache for days and never think about walking five steps to the medicine cabinet and a bottle of aspirin. I used the dishes until there weren't anymore, and then I was surprised when I couldn't find a clean plate. All through grade school, appearance-conscious Wynn was the one who noticed when I needed new shoes.

But I didn't marry George just for his domestic skills. In his own way, George believed in me. "Maud, you can do anything you set your mind to. I know you'll be a great artist someday." In fact, I think George believed in me too much. He could never leave my art alone. He always wanted to help me "make it better." It was his idea to go into the greeting card business. "Money is how our culture measures success, Maud. You don't want to be one of these artists that don't make a dime off your work until after you're dead, do you?" And it was George's idea "to centralize, and thus, focus" my work by containing it in a studio "that would have been the envy of Picasso."

I gave George's stone several more smacks with my boot, rubbed my eyes, gazed out over the other graves. Across the cemetery, an old woman was taking a rubbing from an ancient stone. On her knees, she scrubbed furiously at the headstone, transferring the impressions of the gravestone to paper with a piece of charcoal, while the wind buffeted her, and the leaves rubbed against her legs. She pushed away a lock of thin, grey hair blown into her eyes. The sheet of white paper she was bent over fluttered, and she hurried to grab it.

When I was young, before I got mixed up with husbands and politicians, I made rubbings of leaves with crayons—red, orange, brown, yellow, blue, purple, pink. I stacked them together and stapled them into a book. And, although I made the book in summer when the leaves were green and supple, I called it my autumn book.

I love color. I have no interest in vast amounts of knowledge. George could never understand the way I could pass up a chance at facts, figures, and dates. I like to eat breakfast cereals full of shapes and colors: red balls, pink hearts, yellow stars, purple dinosaurs. George was a cornflakes man. He liked numbers, sure things. You could always count on a spreadsheet. When we sat in Olympic Stadium watching the Montreal Expos play, I was the one who screamed and yelled and demolished hotdogs smothered in mustard and relish. George kept statistics. What looked to me to be a hard-hit grounder through the clumsy third baseman's legs into the green AstroTurf of left field was to George a ground ball to seven with an error on five.

The old woman returned the charcoal to a small fishing tackle box, then carefully rolled the paper and slid it into a cardboard tube. She nodded as she passed us, then began to whistle, something that sounded like the wind, lonely.

I was tired. Granite is harder than the human toe. I slipped to the ground and leaned my head against George's stone. It was hard and perfect and new. I hadn't fazed it, just as I hadn't fazed George in fifteen years of marriage.

Without a word, T-Bone picked me up and carried me to the truck. He settled me gently on the passenger seat. As he drove me home, I swore I'd never speak to George again.

Why do we speak to the dead? Because in death they seem a million times more sympathetic than they were in life. Because we left something unsaid. Because they had filled a hole we didn't even realize was there.

Or maybe just because they still piss us off.

It's over, George. Are you there? George?

Maybe it's because they never let us get the last word in.

2

A Life Like Country Music

Beaver Creek Road dead-ends at my barn. There, the front yard, the drive, and the road all blend together into a part-grass, part-gravel common area. A gathering place for vehicles and equipment and lawn chairs. My house looks down a valley, a tunnel of ever changing color. Full and green in summer. Skeleton black and white in winter. Cider warm brown, gold, and red in autumn. The valley roller-coasters up hills and down all the way to Lake Champlain some thirty miles away.

A writer would say the day was a perfect specimen of Indian summer. The sun has burned off the early morning haze, leaving air so clear and trees so bright that it sends tourists scrambling for their cameras and artists for their easels. I have not broken any records to get to the paints. Standing in my front yard, I watched T-Bone speed to his appointment. He hates being late for anything. He waved as his voice flew out of a cloud of dust and dried leaves, "Get something to eat."

I entered the house and flicked on the radio, navigating through the maze of newspapers, uneaten meals, and discarded clothes. I grabbed a beer from the refrigerator and returned to the front porch, turning up the volume on the radio as I passed. I settled on the sweet spot on the front step, a worn place of music, beer, and sun.

George's funeral was one year ago today.

God, do you remember that day, George? Of course you do. It was your big day. You were the star of the show. Reverend Swan said a lot of nice things about you. It was not an entirely accurate report, but I didn't want to make a scene.

Unlike some people I know.

George and I hadn't had time to get a divorce; at least, I didn't think we had. But the way George's secretary carried on at the funeral, I wasn't sure who was wife and who was just coworker. I had to admit her grief was wholehearted, and the mortician's nephew gave it his all trying to console the wailing woman. I really don't think, like some have whispered, that George had been headed for her when he left me and wrecked himself and our car. To this day, I don't believe it, despite all the clothes and baseball shoes strewn across the road. George loved me; he just couldn't live with me.

The day of the funeral the wind rushed down the mountain and shook the graveside. I shivered and T-Bone put his arm around me. George's secretary wailed louder.

"Why don't you pop that ridiculously bereaved woman in the eye and throw her into the hole with George?" my best friend Freda Lee whispered. "Cynthia Sands on *The Hourglass of Our Lives* would."

I shrugged.

Freda sniffed. "Some secretary. Everyone knew she had the hots for George. Sometimes you are a deep disappointment to me, Maud, a deep disappointment in the romantically aware department." Freda is almost primitive about territorial rights; her husband Lewis Lee is definitely off limits to every other female on the planet.

"Are you eating? You don't look like you're eating." Freda turned to T-Bone. "Is she eating?"

He shrugged.

I said, "I'm trying to get as skinny as Cynthia Sands."

"Very funny," Freda said.

In towns the size of Round Corners, where people practically live inside each other's head, neighbors don't wonder so much at a wife who doesn't cry for her dead husband. Instead, they worry. I should have had George cremated and avoided all the commotion. In all fairness, that's what I should have done after fifteen years of marriage, in which I got burned plenty. When I die, I told Freda, I don't want a funeral, not even a memorial service. I want two lines at the bottom of my obituary: "Friends are welcome at the Round Corners Restaurant between 2 and 4 P.M. Coffee's on Maud."

George the accountant would have liked that. Such a fiscally responsible thing to do. George knew everything there is to know about money. I'm rather helpless about all that budget stuff. I'm still paying off George's coffin, a box I don't even remember choosing. I can't even begin to count how many Maud Calhoun greeting cards I've had to sell to send George off into the hereafter.

The day of the funeral was windy. And when one huge gust hit the graveside, the legs under the casket trembled, swayed, then to everyone's horror, splayed like a collapsed giraffe. The coffin dropped three feet in an instant, forcing the air below it to evict with a big burp. Everyone froze, except the mortician's nephew, who was slinking toward the hearse.

I would have giggled if it hadn't been for the honor guard. They'd arrived that morning, out of the blue, arranged by Odie probably, to carry a fellow veteran on their broad shoulders.

The honor guard, soldiers accustomed to loud noises and surprise attacks, recovered first from the coffin incident. The leader stepped forward and began to fold the flag. End over end, triangle into triangle, until the coffin was bare, civilian again. He marched a geometric path, stopped, and presented the bundle to me. I stared at him. I thought of the flag in the downstairs closet, the flag George flew every holiday. I never flew flags. And now, I had two. T-Bone nudged me. I hesitantly accepted the flag, jumping when the soldier doll snapped to a salute.

For the finale, Reverend Swan carefully removed a saxophone from an old leather case propped against a tree and played taps. The Reverend is sixty years old and does all the yard work himself on the town's white clapboard church. It keeps him limber for the real exercise in his life: music. Reverend Swan played the horn as if he were auditioning for Saint Peter himself.

He arched backward, catering to the music, coaxing it softly from his soul. Before our eyes, he seemed to grow younger, a lithe spirit. His body hunched and folded over the instrument until he and the horn were one, giving birth to the notes, to the music inside him. All he needed was a pair of sunglasses perched above those ballooned cheeks.

The song slipped onto a breeze headed west, and in the ensuing silence I was glad I had chosen the Reverend to play instead of letting Sergeant Whatsisname talk me into a kid with a trumpet. Reverend Swan had to struggle to return mind and soul back to the cemetery. As Reverend Swan became conscious again of his surroundings, his tall, skinny frame, so elastic in performance, straightened, grew stiff. That far-off look left his blue eyes. He slicked back the tufts of hair on the sides of his bald head with long fingers. Returning to reality, obviously, was a Herculean task. The kid with the trumpet and his music would have never left the cemetery. The end would have come in a snap, with a click of the heels.

Finally composed, Reverend Swan approached me, took my hand in both of his, the way preachers always shake hands, sandwich style, and said, "What did you think?"

"I think George would have said you've never played better."

"He did like my horn."

"That was George, patron of the arts."

The Reverend gently turned me away from the casket. "Maud, you know, if there's anything I can do . . ."

I almost giggled again. Reverend Swan was an ineffective man for a preacher. "He has absolutely no powers of persuasion," George used to say. But I've always thought that that was Reverend Swan's charm, so I smiled and gently recaptured my hand. "Anyway," I said, "the saxophone was good."

"I've never used it before, in this manner."

"You ought to keep it in the act."

"You think so?"

"Absolutely."

His face burst into a happy grin, then quickly sobered. He

nodded and left me to field condolences. Everyone stopped and offered a word of sympathy. They did their best to protect me. No one mentioned the crumpled car full of clothes and baseball shoes.

No one mentioned the house.

We are like that: a family. We are entwined, locked together in life and death like battling stags. We have known each other since the first wind blew through Round Corners. They used to save their leftover house paint for me, for my house. Other people's leftovers were part of those pictures that had captivated Raj, my father, even George at first. Other people's leftovers, colors they liked, colors they'd once chosen. A strange bond, leftovers. One not easily or lightly broken.

Freda offered to stay with me. But I pointed her toward her car. Go on, I said; I knew she was scheduled to work a double shift, lunch and dinner, at the Round Corners Restaurant. Freda Lee couldn't afford to miss out on the gratuity windfall that came with the autumn tourist trade. She supported three children and a hypochondriac husband on her meager wages and tips.

"Go on," I told Freda. "I'll be all right." The restaurant would be packed that night with flatlanders who had come to see the leaves peak. Out-of-staters were big tippers. This time of the year there were school supplies and winter coats to be bought and, of course, a Christmas present for husband Lewis Lee. I can't remember the last time Lewis Lee bought Freda a gift, a *real* present, not one of those things he whittles out of clothes-pins. Freda says she gets all the gifts she needs every night in bed with Lewis Lee. I'm glad the guy is good for something.

Everyone offered their sympathies. Frank and Ella Snowden were the last.

Frank ran Snowden's General Store, and Ella was the local postmistress. Both store and postal station were located in a blue wooden clapboard building down the street from the Round Corners Restaurant. It was a convenient setup. In one stop, you could take care of all your shopping needs from soup to stamps.

Ella was the romantic one. She wrote poetry during slow

periods at the post office, which were many. After all, how many stamps can you sell to a town of five hundred people?

"Reverend Swan's saxophone was a nice touch, Maud," said Ella.

"The sax was off-key," Frank said.

Frank would know about the sax since he sang in the barbershop quartet. The quartet practiced every Wednesday night and had gone to state competition twice.

"You think you know everything about music, Mr. Barbershop Quartet," Ella said. "What did you think, T-Bone?"

T-Bone said it might have been a bit flat.

"Well, I don't care," said Ella. She turned to me. "Don't you think there is something so forlorn about the sound of a solo saxophone? It's as if it is trying to communicate with us." She opened her big purse and began rummaging through its contents. "Now, where did I put that notebook? We better get going, Frank. I can feel a poem coming."

Frank rolled his eyes. "I've got some peas to shelve."

Since neither hired any help, they had closed both the store and the postal station to attend George's funeral. Wherever he was, I bet George was preening: He had done what the great Martin Luther King, Jr. couldn't do—shut down a U.S. Post Office without a squawk.

Not bad, George.

The telephone rang. I pushed myself off the porch.

It took a moment to locate the phone. The place has been a mess ever since George left. George was neatness personified. Nothing ever seemed out of place around him. He was like that little boy in the comics who walks around perpetually enveloped in a whirlpool of dust—only just the opposite. George was enclosed in an invisible neatness layer. You could have performed surgery in his office amid the ledgers, it was so sterile. Unlike George's secretary, I had not been encouraged to go there.

I found the telephone jack and reeled in the phone like a catfish.

It was Wynn Winchester.

"Oh, Maud, I probably shouldn't be talking to you in my condition. You know these first months are the most important. That's when the brain forms. Harvey said you would just be thinking about George today. But I told Harvey, 'I'm going to be by Maud's side,' figuratively speaking of course, no matter what morbid vibes might race along the telephone wire and try to tunnel through my uterine wall."

"You're a good friend, Wynn."

"Well, Maud, we *were* in geography together."

Wynn is the only beautician in town. She prides herself on being a career woman, an entrepreneur, and a future working mother. Besides owning her own business, she is three months, one week, and three days pregnant. The countdown is posted daily on a huge chalkboard in the beauty salon. She and Harvey have wanted children practically from the day they met in ninth grade. This is the closest they have come, and the whole town is holding its breath.

For a while, during a two-month spat with Harvey in our sophomore year, she scared me by dating Odie Dorfmann. She was a mousy-brown cheerleader then; now she's a redhead. Odie was three years ahead of us and, in my opinion, too big to date. A football coach's dream, they called him. I never felt safe around Odie; it was as if he might step on me by mistake.

In the end, my intuition was on target: I should have been wary of Odie.

"Well, what do you think of Odie's plan?" Wynn said excitedly. I could almost see her bouncing on the sofa, her red curls bobbing.

"I'm trying not to."

"It's just what you need. Everyone thinks so."

"Everyone ought to mind their own business."

"Now, that's a ridiculous thing to say; you know it's impossible for us to keep our noses out of your business. We just want to see you happy. We had to do something, Maud, we're your friends. This blockage has gone on too long." Blockage.

Sounded intestinal.

Wynn, who not only reads several magazines from cover to cover but watches every talk show zinging across the airwaves, considers herself fluent in all dialects of medical jargon and psychobabble. Death, disease, and dysfunction fascinate her.

"The only blockage is in your head. I don't paint anymore, Wynn. And that's it."

"Now, Maud, don't be that way. Actually," Wynn's voice became softer and less certain, "I thought maybe you might need a model. Do you think there'll be a pregnant woman in your painting, Maud?"

"There *is* no painting, Wynn."

"I could look much more pregnant than I am. We could use pillows or something. Well, you think about it. I don't want to push you. You're the artist."

I sighed, swished the beer can into the trash basket, and pulled another from the fridge.

"Are you still making booties?"

Wynn had won every prize in the county for her knitting. Harvey's sweaters were prettier than Bill Cosby's, people said. It never failed: Every autumn some tourist from New York City ambled into her shop, tripped over her knitting basket, and offered her hundreds of dollars for the sweater she was knitting. Well, Wynn would say, it *was* to be for her husband (who already had a severe case of wool overload). The tourist always left with the sweater, at twice the original offer. Easy Christmas money, Wynn called the negotiations.

She had one particular pair of knitting needles passed down from her grandmother that she called her lucky needles. I could hear them clicking over the phone. Only lucky needles were to be used on the baby's clothes. This baby was so long awaited (Wynn had miscarried twice) that Wynn was giving anything that smacked of bad omen—ladders, black cats, broken mirrors—a wide berth.

"Oh, I've finished those. I'm on to leggings now. I'm trying to steer clear of the basic blues and pinks. Babies are so unpredictable."

"So I've heard," I said.

I stepped over dirty clothes, newspapers, cups of cold coffee,
beer cans. It looked as if a whole family was camped in the living
room instead of one woman. I shrugged and headed upstairs to
the bedrooms. My western boots clicked on the hardwood
floors. George had hated these boots. I wore them with my jeans
stuffed in the top so he had to look at the fancy stitching on the
olive green suede. I used to wear this shirt to bug him, too. It's a
bright blue Hawaiian shirt with yellow parrots on it. George
didn't like parrots; they reminded him of jungles and Vietnam
and enlistment, which he considered his one big mistake in life
(although he never admitted it to best friend and fellow veteran
Odie).

There at the end, I probably did a lot of things to irritate
George.

As I climbed the staircase, I sipped another Rolling Rock. The
beer was sharp and good. It smelled of the backseats of boys'
cars. The radio, as usual, was tuned to Catfish Joe's morning
show. Despite his name, Joe had a good ear for country music. I
began to hum.

Why couldn't the world be like country music: Things hap-
pened to you, you hurt, you cried, then you got up and started
living again. There was endless love and forbidden love and
doomed love in country music, but not talked-about love, not
taken-apart love, not psychoanalyzed love. Country music came
from the land, where everything was simple and straightforward,
where mystery was a gift.

I hated the way I'd begun analyzing everything. I hated
psychology. People who see motives in everything get on my
nerves. Like Wynn. She insisted there had to be a *reason* for
everything. She had a whole theory about George and me and
the house.

The bedrooms were pale places now. No puffed-up Picasso
bulls. Women in soft, sheer gowns would sleep in such rooms.
Women who would dream pretty dreams, who never woke in a

sweat. No wonder I'd begun sleeping downstairs on the couch, in my clothes, with beer on my breath.

From the bedroom window I stared at the faded picture of Milky Way on the barn. The morning sun shone like a spotlight on the old pet's portrait. Egged on by a northern wind, the leaves gossiped on the branches all the way to Lake Champlain, saying a thousand good-byes to each other.

Up and down the one-hundred-mile lake, sailors are pulling their boats up on shore, readying them for winter. In a few months the lake will freeze. The ice fishermen will drive their trucks out on the frozen water and position their funny little huts where the boats had been. The snowmobilers will rip across the glassy surface. The skaters will click and clatter and thump above the fish.

So long summer. So long George.

I wish.

3

I Should Have Voted for Lewis Lee

Some mornings I push the hangover aside, crank my cold van to life in the dark, and drive the one mile to T-Bone's farm—to watch him dance.

Jacques Leon Thibeault, dairy farmer and dancer, never sleeps in. Every morning at four o'clock T-Bone steps out of the house, steaming mug in hand. He crosses the yard in darkness, heading for the circle of warm, welcoming light cast by the lamp over the barn door. Inside the barn, he flips on more lights, hangs his denim jacket on a hook, and drains his coffee cup. He switches on the radio.

The milk room, where the milk is stored and waits to be transported to the dairy for processing, smells of pine, ammonia, linoleum, and starched linen. Nurses' shoes would squeak across the smooth concrete floor. Everything in the room—bulk tank, sinks, jars, buckets, milk lines—is either glass or stainless steel, sparkling glass and spotless stainless steel. A germ could see itself in the shiny surfaces.

Through a door on the far side is the main section of the barn, a cavernous open area filled with bawling bovines. This is a clean place, too, although it doesn't smell like it. Once a reporter from Burlington wrote an article, "The Vermont Dairy Farmer: A Dying Breed?" The writer made much of the muck and mud, the plodding progress of owner and beast, and the aroma of the barn. He wrote of being "slapped by the smell of cow." T-Bone loves that pungent punch. It is home hitting him in the face.

Like a doctor, T-Bone begins by making rounds. He whistles as he strolls between the rows of stalls. Occasionally, he stops and talks to a cow, examines it more closely, his calm hands traveling knowledgeably over neck and flank, then, with a pat on the rump, he continues to the next cow. When he has traversed the whole of the long barn, and is satisfied with the health and happiness of his sixty head, he begins hooking up the milkers.

Other farmers' cows let down their milk when they hear the bawl of a calf or the hum of the milking machine. T-Bone's cows become stimulated at the sound of his tapping boots. Shuffle, kick, shuffle, kick, udders tingle. Shuffle, kick, milk rushes to the teats.

That morning I pulled up just as T-Bone turned up the volume on the radio. I heard the music swell into the barn, wrap itself around the cows and their udders, and squeeze. As I stepped into the barn, I took in the comfortingly familiar scene. Tails swished. Milk flowed. Feet flew. The bottoms of T-Bone's big rubber boots, which had taps nailed to them, clicked across the concrete as he hoofed from holstein to holstein.

Everyone in the county knew of T-Bone's cows. They were consistent milk producers, and they always gave Grade A milk. The other farmers teased T-Bone: When was he going to call those agriculture boys at the University of Vermont to measure the effects of a floor show on dairy cows?

Dancing had nothing to do with it, T-Bone told them. It was the music. Music relaxes the cows. Cows aren't so different from people, he said.

Leaning against the doorjamb, the collar of my woolen jacket turned up against the autumn snap, I watched T-Bone and began to feel my nerves unwind. It was easy to sneak up on T-Bone while he was dancing. He was oblivious to everything. I knew the feeling; somewhere inside me, some muscle and bone remembered. But it eludes me, like T-Bone. I have never been able to paint T-Bone. I have made a thousand sketches of him. Not one is T-Bone. He is my one great artistic failure. I wish I could give him up. But I keep coming back.

The music lifted, floating up to the top of the barn, which seemed as high as a cathedral. T-Bone tapped and tapped. He was in a trance, in some kind of spiritual experience, a whirling scarecrow in flannel shirt, blue jeans, and Montreal Expos baseball hat. He was marvelous and when the milking was done and the show was over, I clapped my hands. He gasped for breath, now sweating in his long johns and flannel shirt, and smiled at me like a small, shy flower.

When I am at T-Bone's house, he always feeds me. It could be the middle of the afternoon or the middle of the night and he'd insist a four-course meal is no trouble.

While T-Bone cooked pancakes, scrambled eggs, and sausage on the iron stove, I set the table. On the table were a pitcher of milk from T-Bone's cows, butter made from that same milk, maple syrup from T-Bone's trees, and cinnamon rolls baked by T-Bone. Muffins, croissants, French bread, coffee cake, rolls. Anything with yeast, flour, and butter is right up T-Bone's culinary alley. He took up the kitchen detail at a young age; his uncle André had been the worst cook in Canada.

The hotcakes disappeared as we silently traded sections of the newspaper. T-Bone devoured the news, from front to back, every headline and dateline. Car bombing, nine dead. Plane crash, one hundred sixty-seven dead. Price supports, dead. Summit talks, believed dead. American farmers, dead or dying. It was enough food to fuel a worrier of his caliber for a month. But T-Bone breezed through the paper immune to catastrophe and mayhem.

Spending the morning with his cows and his dancing was, for T-Bone, like going to church or being downwind of a bonfire of burning marijuana. He was untouchable, protected by the euphoria that sang along his nerves and the peace that settled softly upon his spirit like a billowing blanket. As the day wore on and the experience wore off, he would begin to worry again, stewing over me and milk prices and what those idiot politicians in Washington would do next. But for now, he was whole and happy. Salvation seemed as close as the milk jug at his elbow. When he was like this, I wanted to burrow close to his peaceful aura like a small animal seeking shelter from the winter wind. His calm seemed as real as concrete, capable of withstanding the battering of Odie's tenacity, Wynn's well-meaning nagging, and all the other guilt-laden vibes I had been receiving from the community lately.

I sipped at my coffee. T-Bone did not believe in beer for breakfast.

"I'm afraid," I said, "they're not going to leave this alone."

He gathered the dishes, took them to the sink, and ran hot, sudsy water over them. His strong arms dived into bubbles up to the elbow. The muscles in his forearms worked as he sponged a plate clean of syrup and pancake crumbs, rinsed it, and stacked it in the rubber dish drainer. I collected a red-checkered dish towel dangling from the refrigerator handle, snatched the slick plate, and began to dry.

"I haven't painted in years, not real painting like I used to do," I said.

"Years."

"It's not like I don't want to paint. They think all I have to do is want it. That isn't enough."

"So tell them."

"I have!"

"What are they going to do? Tie you to your easel?"

"Of course not."

"Maybe they'll blackmail you. Unearth some indecent Maud Calhoun greeting cards."

"Don't be absurd."

T-Bone washes dishes just as Wynn and I were taught in home economics. Glassware, silverware, plates first before the water turns too greasy, then pots and pans, the kitchen equipment that seldom touches the human mouth. When I wash dishes, I never pay attention to the order of things. I grab whatever is nearest to the sink. Wynn and the instructor used to shake their heads in despair during those silly practice sessions in the home ec room's tidy little kitchenette. They said I showed a shocking dis-regard for kitchen protocol. I said the white kitchenette needed some color, maybe an avocado refrigerator for starters.

T-Bone finished the last pan, a heavy cast-iron skillet, plucked the stopper from the drain, dried his hands, and headed for the office at the back of the big, old farmhouse.

I trailed behind him.

His office is the cleanest, warmest corner of the house. No dust demons or rattling wind here. Actually, this long, spacious room started as three little rooms. But, like any true Vermonter, T-Bone couldn't leave them alone. He knocked down walls, threw up big sturdy cathedral-like pine beams across the ceiling, lined the walls with bookcases. Books, magazines, a complex stereo system I can't even figure how to turn on, odds and ends—everything from a pinecone to a sample bottle of cow vitamins—run the length and height of three walls. The fourth wall is a wall of windows. They bring the outdoors in, the woods, the path, the birdhouse. The room has a woodstove, sofa, and Cat. A computer hums on the desk. Agriculture magazines are piled knee-high in the corner.

At night T-Bone reads on the sofa because he likes being near the cat and this is the only room the cat likes. He reads whatever he grabs from the shelf, Jane Austen, W. Somerset Maugham, Zen. He has a weakness for Kerouac because he thinks Kerouac might have liked my old house. But, T-Bone said, he was glad Kerouac never passed my house. Kerouac surely would have stopped and started writing on the spot, going on and on as the pictures once had gone on and on with no beginning and no end. Yes, T-Bone said, he was lucky that Kerouac never saw the house, that Kerouac and I had never met.

T-Bone had loved my house, too. He was the only one who never asked: "What is this supposed to be?" or "Why did you draw that?" Unlike George, he knew the paintings were just vehicles to a place inside me—streetcars to self-definition. I believe we all have those places, and, for some reason, we can't keep ourselves from trying to get there. What happens when we get lost and we can't find the road to creativity? We talk to dead husbands and spend our paychecks on Rolling Rock.

"No ropes, no guns, no blackmail. Then what's your problem?" T-Bone said, settling behind the desk.

"I love them."

"Ah." He tapped on the computer keys and studied the screen. Some of the cows were due for vaccinations that week. He must remember to call the vet, he said. As if he would forget.

"I mean, in a way, they're family. Families always think they know what's best for you, and they aren't shy about telling you what it is." I flung myself on the sofa, bouncing off the cat. "Odie's already given me a check for the supplies. And yesterday Reverend Swan dropped by with a cassette tape of 'inspirational sax.' To help me get in the mood, he said."

"Don't worry," T-Bone frowned at the computer screen and mumbled distractedly. "It'll all work out."

I glared at him. "You're a real pain in the ass when you're mellow."

The traffic stopped, started, stopped again. I love sugar maples, I adore birches, I ogle oaks, but I sure wouldn't drive two hundred miles to see their leaves die.

The trees crawled past the window of my ancient green van, which was as exasperated with the pace as I was. It choked and rattled, scowled and threatened to dump me in the middle of nowhere with a hundred pounds of dead engine. The van and I hate people who ride the brake.

Twenty minutes. Forty minutes. An hour late. While Freda wore down the thick soles of her white, orthopedic shoes at the Round Corners Restaurant ("You think I'm going to let my arches drop? I'm taking care of myself for Lewis Lee"), I was stuck in the funeral march of the leaf peakers.

It always amazes me that humans, who mix every conceivable color in their chemistry labs, seem astounded when nature manages to produce a hue other than green. I wouldn't mind if they came because they truly loved the fiery reds, burnt oranges, and flaming yellows. I understand the uplifting quality of color. But, I suspect, the real reason the autumn people storm New

England, as the bourgeoisie did the guillotine, is for the show, the chance to see a good aristocratic head roll. Their friends told them they really must see New England in autumn. The Experience was everything, according to the cocktail party circuit. It gives people something to chat about. Police see it all the time at auto accidents and fires. Today, half the Vermont countryside was burning and drawing a crowd.

They clogged usually deserted roads like mine. They came from big cities to the south and French cities to the north, loaded with enough camera equipment to keep Japan in business—two migrations of shutterbugs colliding in the hills and valleys of Vermont. They crept along the roads in every form of vehicle, motorcycle, big car, and bus. They stopped without giving notice and pulled out without looking. They made U-turns on narrow roads, curves, and hills.

"Oh, Harold, I want a picture of that one." Snap. Click. Crash. "Harold, why don't you watch where you're going?"

"May I see your license, please?"

All to watch a few million leaves die.

Round Corners's one real street—the only one with a center line maintained thanks to the state's paint crew—is known as Highway 100 on the Vermont state map. Usually it was sufficient for the small town's needs. However, it was not nearly enough highway for the hundreds of tourists who passed through on a bright, musty-smelling fall afternoon.

Since finding a parking space on the street would be impossible for the next two weeks, I automatically whipped in behind Wynn's Cut and Curl.

Wynn Winchester was knitting. She sat under one of the shop's two hair dryers, the bubble hood of the dryer flipped up. From the basket at her feet, I surmised the mysterious tangle of yarn dangling from her lucky needles was going to be a red sweater for Junior. A tiny sleeve hung over the edge of the knitting basket. "Wynn, I'm parked behind your place, OK?" I said, poking my head in the shop. The bell over the door jingled.

"Might as well. All the traffic has shot my business today. People don't want to kick and claw their way to a perm. As if I could give anyone a nice curl even if they were feeling energetic."

"Still having morning sickness, huh?"

Wynn motioned to a shelf of bottles and spray cans. "The stuff makes me sicker than a dog." The hairdresser sighed, then suddenly brightened. She smiled and stretched her shirt tight across her stomach. "I think I'm starting to show. What do you think?"

I shrugged. "Looks like it to me."

"There. I'll tell that to the High and Mighty Harvey Winchester. He thinks I'm nuts, but husbands don't know a thing. No matter how many of those baby books they read. A woman knows when she's starting to show." Harvey had been studying baby books ever since they learned Wynn was pregnant. He was a fount of information on breast feeding, the formative years, and ear infections.

"How long do Harvey's books say this morning sickness is supposed to last?"

"Harvey's books say I'll be out of the woods in another month. The doctor concurs. Until then, the women of Round Corners are just going to have to do without their fancy hair care."

I shivered. Things could get ugly around here.

I crossed the street to the Round Corners Restaurant. As usual, the first thing I did upon entering the restaurant was inspect the cash register. The supply of Maud Calhoun greeting cards was low. Barns, mountains, cows. The tourists loved them, just as George said they would. I found a red crayon at the bottom of my purse and wrote MORE CARDS on an order pad, ripped off the sheet, and stuffed it in my pocket.

The bell over the restaurant door jangled behind me. I quickly stashed my purse and jacket in a cabinet under the cash register. Two men squeezed their bulky shapes onto stools at the horseshoe-shaped counter. I poured coffees—one black and one with cream—and set them before Amos and Bartholomew. "After-noon, boys."

Freda, already making dinner salads in the kitchen, poked her head over the top of the swinging doors. "Maud Calhoun, you're late, as usual."

"Traffic."

Freda pursed her lips and went back to filling salad bowls. "You look like hell," she mumbled. "You need to lay off the Rolling Rock."

I ignored her, leaning on the swinging doors. "Been busy?"

"Watching leaves is hungry business."

"Good for tips," I said, tying on a white polyester apron. "Had to park behind Wynn's today; she's not doing any perms for a while. The smell gets to her."

"Damn!" Freda patted her hair. She wore it swept up in the back, cascading into a fall of curls. She hated her straight, blonde hair and always said she'd die without a regular perm. Her husband, Lewis Lee, had never seen her without a curl in her hair. "By the time Wynn gets over morning sickness, I'll look like something on the side of the road."

This latest prenatal inconvenience hardly affected me. I was told my mother's black curls had swarmed around her head like bees. I liked to think that she hadn't been able to control her hair either. My hair gave everything the slip—barrettes, bobby pins, braids. But to keep the health department happy, I kept trying to strong-arm my curls into obedience with a coated rubber band.

"Well, you won't be the only one in town," I said tucking a curl behind my ear.

Harping again on my haggard features and bloodshot eyes, Freda said, "We'll all look like you. Shit."

The Round Corners Restaurant could have been made from a kit. You could have set it up anywhere in the country, at any intersection of civilization and wild, weary highway, at any meeting place of greasy spoon and gasoline. It would have looked, smelled, operated the same. Speckled Formica tabletops, large Woolworth landscapes, high vinyl booths, plastic flowers, sugar and NutraSweet packages on the tables. If you needed to know the hours of the Round Corners Savings and Loan down the street, you consulted the ashtray. If you wanted a florist or needed an undertaker, you perused the back of the menu under the disclaimer: "Sponsorship of this menu is no reflection on the quality of the establishment's wares."

Since the restaurant was the only entertainment in town, all romance in Round Corners was carried on there. Boys usually brought their girls to the restaurant on the first date. Couples celebrated their engagement, wedding, and anniversaries at the Round Corners Restaurant. It was there lovers quarreled over the pork tenderloin and made up over the smothered steak. It was perhaps there that she first saw his eyes wander to someone else or he heard she was moving in with Mother.

Clientele was skiers in winter, leaf peakers in fall, summer people in summer, and Amos and Bartholomew all the time. Their wives complain that they live at the Round Corners Restaurant. They drink so much coffee they keep Brazil in business. Sometimes they sit all day on the same stool, some- times (depending on the season and the weather) they leave half a cup standing to head into the woods and chop trees or nail down somebody's roof or feed the stove in the sugar shack. Year after year the country's economic muscle flops and flexes, but Amos and Bartholomew work no more and no less.

"Heard they put you on the map, Maud," Bartholomew said. The Vermont Department of Tourism had distributed this year, for the first time, fifty thousand copies of *The Guide to Leaf Peaking in the Green Mountain State.* My road was number seventeen on the list.

I nodded. "I've never seen so many crazy drivers in my life. And they're all turning around in my drive."

"Reminds me of my kid's ant farm," Amos said.

"I can't believe the tourism department is rating the color of my trees." I refilled their cups. "Why don't they hire buses? Set up a stand? Sell T-shirts?"

"That's Montpelier for you," Bartholomew said.

"That's the whole world," Amos said.

"That's a fact," they huffed. "Bureaucrats." Amos and Bartholomew had no great love for government, state or federal.

As Freda said, watching leaves was hungry business. The dinner crowd didn't let up the entire shift. We ran out of baked potatoes first, then filet mignon and 7UP. The list of what we didn't have became longer than what we did have. And still the people came, from the North and the South and a bean farm in Ohio. They came and we served and the kid who calls himself the cook complained.

"Quiche? What kind of place do they think this is? I don't read French; I don't cook French. What is this *pomme frites,* shit, Maud? French fries? That I can handle."

The special for the day was hamburger steak, mashed potatoes, and lima beans, so I was not surprised when Frank and Ella Snowden slid into a booth by the window. Hamburger steak was Frank's favorite.

Frank liked to sit with his back to the wall, so he could watch the door, he said. Ella always let him have his way, although, she said, she didn't know who he expected to sneak up on them, Jesse James maybe, or some other desperado. I didn't even bother to offer menus, just poured them two coffees and, five minutes later, plunked two specials in front of them.

"Bon appetit."

"Maud," Ella said, shaking out the paper napkin on her lap. "I've been wondering about this mural."

I sighed and leaned my hip against the booth.

"I mean, I've been thinking what it needs is a nice little verse. Something typed up and hung beside it, the way they do in museums, sort of a poetic description."

"Ella, I haven't agreed to paint the mural."

"But you must. We all know you can do it."

"It's been a long time."

"Posh. Like riding a bicycle. Isn't it, Frank?"

Frank concentrated on his hamburger steak.

"Well, it is," Ella said. "You've just been a little lost the last few years what with your father dying and then George. None of us likes to see you like this, Maud. While I'm the first to admit Sheriff Odie Dorfmann is no reservoir of original thought, he had a good one this time. It was a godsend, and we're not going to sit and let you pass it by."

"Who's 'we'? You got fleas?" Frank said.

Ella glared at him.

I massaged my forehead. A headache with the rhythm of a jackhammer had been excavating my cranium all night. "I don't know why everyone thinks they know what's good for me."

"We care for you," Ella said.

"Ella, she doesn't have to do it if she doesn't want to." Frank put down his fork. "You shouldn't force her."

"I'm not *forcing* her. I would never *force* her. Maud's like a daughter to me, Frank, and you know it."

Frank's expression softened slightly. They had no children of their own. "You could write your poem even if she doesn't paint the damn mural."

"But this would be my first published work, well, sort of published on a wall."

I touched her arm. "I really don't think I can do it."

Ella removed her arm from my touch. "You used to not be so hard, Maud."

I glanced helplessly at Frank. He nodded at me.

I sighed and left their table, passing Wynn and Harvey Winchester in the next booth. Harvey had five baby books piled on the table. He was so busy explaining to Wynn the purpose of measuring cranium size in babies that he dipped a french fry in his drinking water instead of the ketchup; he slid the soggy fry between his teeth without noticing.

In the kitchen, I headed for the storage room in the back. There, hanging on the wall, was a mirrored, white metal medicine chest. In the chest were aspirin. I sat on a fifty-pound bag of potatoes and swallowed two pills without water.

George, what am I going to do?

"You could get off your caboose and serve these fucking

pomme frites, Maud," the cook yelled.

Five minutes to closing, a family of ten filed in and slid onto stools. There was a father and so many children they wrapped around the counter. The littlest looked to be around five. The oldest was a skinny boy with a face full of pimples. A younger brother on the stool next to him whispered something in his ear. He nodded and said, "In a minute." They studied the menu, then, without a word exchanged, the father ordered one special and ten orders of fries. All ten reluctantly closed the menus. The oldest boy grabbed his brother's hand and headed in the direction of the rest rooms.

"Drinks?" I said.

"Water'll be fine."

I turned in the order ("Again with the fries," said the cook) and brought the water.

"Passing through?" I asked.

The man finished off his water in one gulp and nodded. I replenished his glass. "Thanks."

"Well, it's a nice time of year for it. Where you from?"

"West. Ohio."

"We had a bean farm," said one of the children.

"We're going to be Mainiacs," said another.

"Sally!" said the weary father.

"So you're headed for Maine," I said.

"Yes, ma'am."

I glanced out the window. Their car, an old station wagon with Ohio license plates, was covered with dust. Murdered insects dangled from the grill and splattered the windshield. You couldn't see out of the dirty back window, the car was so crammed with suitcases, pillows, and toys. There was no room for nine children.

I strode into the kitchen and told the smart-aleck cook to give me nine more specials. "Nine! In case you hadn't noticed, Maud, I'm trying to clean up. It'll be Christmas by the time I get this steam table closed down. And I got a date tonight."

"Ten specials in all, Casanova."

The weary father tried to argue. "Don't be silly," I said. "It would have all gone to waste anyway. Vermont's health department regulations are murder on leftovers."

When the family was finished, I gave the father directions to Reverend Swan's house. "He can put you up for the night. He won't preach at you too much, but you might have to listen to his saxophone."

The Round Corners Restaurant closed at eleven. It was Freda's turn to mop. I gathered all the sugar containers on a tray, took them to a booth, and began filling them. Freda finished the floor first and plopped in the booth across the table from me. I screwed the lid on the last sugar container, and we both swung our legs up on the seat and leaned back. Freda lit a cigarette.

"Lewis Lee wants me to quit these things." She frowned at the cigarette.

"Wouldn't be a bad idea."

She rested her head against the wall and blew a long stream of smoke, obviously thoroughly enjoying the cigarette. "You still mulling over Odie's cultural mission?"

"I don't know why he didn't run on a law and order platform like any normal sheriff and town selectman."

"A civilized populace is less likely to kill each other."

"As history has proven again and again," I said, massaging my neck. "I wish I hadn't voted for him."

Freda tapped the ash from her cigarette. "I always go for the write-in candidate. Every election I vote for Lewis Lee."

4

Cows Juggling Pinecones

About a week ago, I began painting cows.

This is what it's come to, George. Look what you've done to me.

Udderly ridiculous. Cute, George. Tell Jack Benny he's got nothing to worry about.

Cows in baseball uniforms, pregnant cows, preaching cows, but still cows. Cows with spots, cows lying on couches, cows in trees. Lost cows. Cows taken to market, to the cleaners, for a ride. Cows eating spaghetti, cows blowing on saxophones, cows at a slaughterhouse choosing human livers and tongues. It ceased to be amusing after the third day.

It's a cow, George. I know it's wearing a bikini and flip-flops.

The cows were the most recent setback in my continuing struggle with paint and canvas. For years, I have followed the same routine. Perched ramrod straight on a stool in my studio, I face the canvas. The door is locked. I am alone with a white surface of relatively small proportions. In a few hours, its blankness will grow to overwhelming dimensions like one of those baby bathtub dinosaurs that turn into Godzilla in the fish tank. Today, in an effort to head off Godzilla, I created the Hatteras Holstein.

I drummed my fingers on the nearby table. In the quiet studio, country music lovesickness wandered out of the radio in decibels guaranteed to damage the human ear. The studio, which is in the attic at the top of the house, vibrated to the beat of lonely hearts, cheatin' hearts, achy breaky hearts. I imagined I heard a faucet dripping below, three flights down. I unlocked the door and ran

down the stairs to check it. While I was in the kitchen, I drank a
glass of water. I peered at the thermometer outside the win-
dow—forty-five degrees. I loaded the dishwasher. I considered
washing the windows and cleaning underneath the refrigerator
but decided that was going too far. I could not avoid it. I had to
return to the attic. And sure enough, the cow was still there,
sunning in all that bright blank canvas. Everything was exactly as
I left it—waiting.

I glanced at the clock. Two more hours to go, one hundred
and twenty minutes until I could stop. George and I agreed that
to give my work a fair chance, I ought to spend mornings in the
studio. No interruptions. Turn the answering machine on.
Forget about any work around the house. Until high noon.

*I don't know why I'm still following your stupid rules,
George. I suppose I don't know what else to do.*

Poor George. He was right to leave. He got out while the
getting was good. I was impossible to live with, still am.

It needs sunglasses? You could be right, George.

*What does it mean? It doesn't mean anything. Everything
doesn't have to mean something. God, you're as bad as
Wynn. You think too much.*

*What else is there to do, where you are? I don't know; take
up a hobby.*

There. That's what I mean. I was married to George for fif-
teen years, and each year I grew more and more unpleasant. A
grizzly with a thumbtack in its paw would have been better
company. I was never malicious or cruel. I was just . . . irrever-
ent. I couldn't seem to take anything, especially George, seri-
ously. For example, I almost died laughing when he suggested I
make a will.

"Everyone should have a will, Maud, for the disposition of
property," according to George. I remember the morning. I
couldn't keep my eyes off the clock. That day I had awakened
with a feeling, an urge to get up to the attic. I felt, almost, as if I
could paint.

"George, we're young. We've got plenty of time." I tapped my fingers on the counter, checked the clock again.

"It's never too early, when it comes to taxes or wills. What if we both die at the same time? Fall off the Appalachian Trail into a ravine and freeze to death. You don't want the state to get everything, do you?"

"If I'm a Popsicle, who cares? George . . ." I glanced at the clock. George had installed an institutional-looking timepiece over the kitchen sink. He said kitchens always had clocks; how else could you tell how long to boil the pasta?

"And if we go separately, without wills, things could be tied up in the courts forever. Lawyers' fees would eat you alive."

"Then I wouldn't need the will, would I? Sorry, George, I've really got to go." I ran from the kitchen and up the back stairs, tripping over my own feet. I skidded around corners, fumbled with doorknobs. But, when I reached the studio, found a brush, set up the canvas, plopped on the stool, and pushed my hair out of my eyes . . . the feeling was gone.

I came to think of George as a thief. He stole moments. And hearts. Sometimes I wonder what I saw in George. And then I remember how charming he could be, how his voice soothed people like Ella when she became harried and forgetful during the Christmas rush.

George had ambition and a great body that moved with a planned quickness, like a stalking puma. I think he had political aspirations (although he never admitted to it and never actually set his sights higher than town moderator). In a calculated way, he wanted to be liked. And I didn't help him a bit. I got drunk during his speech at the annual convention of the New England Association of Accountants and Tax Preparers. I never wore the correct clothes. (I was the only woman at the convention in black leather.) I wanted to make love at all the wrong times (such as in the elevator after the tax speech). George only made love at night, in the dark, on Tuesdays and Thursdays. Or so it seemed. Actually, we probably made love on the occasional Wednesday or Friday, but for the life of me I can't remember a time. I only remember his voice.

His voice, when he talked to me, always had a patient quality: "Now, Maud, you know that is inappropriate behavior." Sesame Street jive. I deserved it, of course. I was horrible and lazy and worthless. George took over the cooking, mastering the gadgets he bought for me—the food processor and microwave oven and pasta maker. He read their instructions to the last letter. Manuals were George's idea of bedtime reading. "You know, Maud, if we had a large enough microwave, we could probably defrost a whole cow in less than three minutes."

He wanted, more than anything, for me to be a great painter. "Realize your ambitions, Maud," he said, standing surveillance over a bag of popcorn expanding its horizons in the microwave. He sniffed the air, which was filled with the warm smell of butter, and smiled. "Ambition is like the microwave; it radiates the inside and, soon, you're cooking."

George encouraged me to spend hours at my art. If George had a fault, it was that he was too helpful. He organized my work space. Once it spread wildly about the farm like some kind of growing thing. George contained it in the attic studio. It was a dream studio. There were shelves and jars for everything. George cut a hole in the roof and put in a special window that let the light pour in from the sky; it was cathedral light, holy light.

It was perfect.

And impossible to work in. I spent all morning in there, until George came home for lunch. I listened to him start lunch, throwing the pork chops into the microwave. (George believed there wasn't anything you couldn't microwave.) And when I descended the stairs to gnaw on those chops with the mixed-up molecules, George knew by my expression it had been an unproductive morning. "Cheer up, Maud, you'll get it right tomorrow," he said. "I know you will."

"Probably." I pushed aside the glass of milk he had poured and fetched a beer from the refrigerator.

He was so patient. He should have left me much sooner than he did. I know he was tempted, especially during my criminal period. There was a time when I stole things. It lasted only a few months, at a time when I couldn't even draw cows, and I was never caught. I took little things that I never remembered taking.

George liked to drive into Burlington and catch the red-light specials at one of the discount department stores. But for a while there, maybe six months, whenever we walked out of the store, I found things in the pockets of my parka. Little digital alarm clocks that you stick on the dashboard of the car, earrings (clip-ons, not even pierced), a bottle of calamine lotion.

"Where did you get those, Maud?" George asked in his patient, grating voice.

"I don't know. They seem to have just appeared in my pocket. Like magic."

"There is no such thing as magic, Maud."

The shoplifting never amounted to much, and George kept down the proceeds by holding my hand in the store. We strolled through cosmetics, shoes, hardware, from one red-light special to another, looking like lovers, avoiding crime. Petty larceny didn't shake George's cool.

Actually, the only time he ever lost his temper with me, the only time I ever went against his wishes, was when I took the job at the Round Corners Restaurant. I became a waitress because it gave me an excuse not to be an artist. Although I still entered the attic every morning and played chicken with a white piece of canvas, my life didn't revolve around cows in flip-flops anymore (or their equivalent subject matter back then). I expanded my horizons to cooked cow: smothered steak and filet mignon.

George disliked my new career move because it wasn't "furthering my artistic goals," as he put it, and because it was there I met Freda Lee. Freda Lee irritated George with her talk of soap operas and afternoon sex with Lewis Lee. She was so busy having fun with Lewis Lee, she was oblivious to the other things that made the world go around—the depression, the anger, the deviousness. I liked her immediately.

Lewis Lee was the center of her life, her focus, her salvation. She supported him and three children on what she made at the restaurant. Lewis Lee seldom worked. Everyone, except Freda,

called him lazy. Lewis was not a well man, she said. And he had
the paperwork to prove it. Lewis Lee always found a doctor
somewhere to swear he was sick at the very least or possibly
dying. One time he had to travel all the way to Boston (and in his
condition) for a reasonably poor prognosis. Still, Lewis Lee was
Freda's life. He was the air she breathed. And, in my mind, that
was job enough.

Freda's sensuality slid over her body, fitting her tiny waist and
lush hips; it whispered, like her tight polyester waitress uniform,
as she walked. She fascinated men with her blonde hair, soft
skin, and easygoing temperament. She laughed, turned down
their offers, dodged the occasional wandering hand. It wouldn't
occur to her to take them seriously. She was so wrapped up in
Lewis Lee she wasn't even aware she was flashing signals hot
enough to melt the sky on a cold, snowy night.

George considered Freda a bad influence, contributing to my
already tenuous grasp on respectability. "Don't be so stuffy," I
told George, balancing a large, glossy coffee-table book (*The
Joy of Impressionism,* I think) on my head. Since the impres-
sionism text was no great challenge, I also juggled four pine-
cones. Pinecones were tricky. The spikes, you know.

George did not juggle, and the only books he balanced were
his clients'. He was particular about appearances, his clothes, his
ideas. He hated to wear the same pair of underwear two days in
a row when I forgot the laundry. And he cringed when I became
loud at softball games.

"Kill the sucker, George! All right! No batter no batter no
batter. Wooooeeee!" George sought dignity even in spikes. We
drove home from those games, George staring straight out the
windshield, tight-lipped; me coming down from that boy-did-we-
slaughter-them high and miserably remembering all the rotten
things I'd said about the other team's mothers.

"I don't know what you want, Maud," George said in a de-
feated voice.

I was silent. Apologies, by then, had dubious value.

"You know I want you to be happy, Maud." More Sesame

Street therapy. "I want you to be the best you can be."

That was the attitude that got me in my present predicament.

George the patron saint of the arts was 150 percent behind Odie Dorfmann's reelection plans. They plotted the entire campaign together during an Expos game in our living room. Odie was always at our house either talking or watching baseball. He was the pitcher of the Round Corners Royals softball team; George was the third baseman.

One night while the Montreal Expos were kicking butt, Odie announced his campaign plans for reelection. He leaned forward, looking us in the eyes, and whispered, "Culture." That was Odie's campaign strategy. He was going to bring not only leadership, but culture to Round Corners. This was about the time the *Burlington Free Press* ran an article on the explosion of the arts scene in Vermont.

When I told Freda the next day after work, she couldn't take it. She laughed so hard she almost fell out of the booth, where we were sprawled, tired and dirty. The doors were locked, and we smelled of hamburgers. There were two sodas on the table and an ashtray. "Culture," Freda sighed, wiping the tears from the corners of her eyes and lighting a cigarette. "It's good Odie is sticking to something he knows."

George died shortly before Odie was elected. Odie took it hard. He and George had met in Vietnam, two scared, green kids with faces full of pimples and a shared love of baseball. At night as they listened to bombs in the distance, they whispered baseball statistics to each other. George had been visiting his old army buddy Odie the day I met him.

In the aftermath of losing his best friend and winning his second term, Odie forgot about his cultural mission. Until now. Our period of mourning was over, as was half of Odie's second term. Even Odie can figure out a calendar. And the issue of the Round Corners mural was heating up. People liked the idea. When they talked about the painting—what it would look like and who would be in it—they discovered they felt closer to each other. "What about that painting" became the popular greeting, comparable to sports salutations such as "What about those Bosox" or "What about those Expos" (depending on your baseball persuasion). The concept of the painting grew in the town's mind. Odie envisioned something the size of a city block while the last thing I had done with any confidence—the greeting cards—was no bigger than a brick. You could say I was feeling the pressure.

George had been oblivious to pressure. "A person can do anything he wants to or can afford," he said, straightening his tie and heading out the door for the closing of a house. I remember the day because it was the biggest house George had sold yet. He was extremely proud of that transaction. "Maud," he said, "this is a Renoir of a real estate deal."

The irony of the situation was that Odie wouldn't lose the election if he didn't produce a town mural. My spiteful side was denied even that satisfaction. The voters weren't irate. They wouldn't feel cheated if their cultural consciousness wasn't raised another notch. And if they did, what choice do they have? Odie was running unopposed, again.

So I should have been able to tell Odie to stick that painting where the sun doesn't shine—in his L.L. Bean thermal under-wear.

What's stopping me, George? I'll tell you what's stopping me . . . It's the look of excitement everyone gets in their eyes when they talk about the mural . . . It's this sense of bonding that has begun to permeate the town . . . It isn't my mural . . . It's theirs.

Everyone wants a piece of this dream. They say it will put Round Corners on the map again. For once, people will stop here for more than a hamburger between downhill ski runs or for a break from heavy-duty leaf peaking. They'll come to see the mural.

Just like they once came to see my house.

I leaned back and studied the painting in front of me. I had put away the Hatteras Holstein and started again. The new painting was beginning to look suspiciously like another cow, only this one had two heads.

What does it look like I'm doing, George? You're dead, not blind.

Of course it's not right. I don't know how to fix it, George; if I did, I would. Yes. It's a good thing I still have those cute little greeting cards. The tourists love them just as you said they would. Now go away. Please? What do you mean what is that red glob in the middle? George . . . George? George come back here and explain. Damn, you always do this to me. If you weren't already dead, I'd probably kill you.

T-Bone once told me his dancing was like a thing clawing inside him to get out. If he didn't listen to it, he said, it would destroy him. There was something inside me lately, tearing, mad, slashing through arteries, muscle, and organ. I studied the softly forming cow and gave in to all the despair and heartache and frustration. I hurt inside and cried from the pain. Little sniffles at first. Then mighty sobs. I couldn't watch another cow birth. I raised my hand to my eyes. It was dripping with blood.

Great.

On the floor was a shattered jar, and on the table where I had slammed my hand through the glass was the red imprint of my palm.

Downstairs someone was pounding on the front door. I wrapped paper towels around my hand until it looked like a huge paper paw and answered the door. "I don't want any."

The man standing on the porch smiled.

"Look, I've got my hands full right now and . . ."

He glanced at the paw, which was reddening, soaking up blood faster than spilled coffee in a television commercial. The smile slipped. The man promptly turned green, folded into a pretzel, and threw up.

5

A Picture of Thomas Looking for Pictures

His name was Thomas. And he came here looking for the pictures.

"What happened to the house?" he asked, driving back from the doctor's office.

"The house?" I said.

He thrust a photograph under my nose. Unthinkingly, I took it with my bandaged hand and winced. The local anesthesia was wearing off. I needed a Rolling Rock; make that six.

The photograph was a picture of my house taken years ago when it had been swimming in scenes and portraits. A man stood in front of the house, smiling. He had blonde hair, down to his shoulders, scraped back from his face with a leather head-band. He wore scruffy jeans, a work shirt, and love beads. I knew by the composition that the photo had been taken by my father; it was shot from a slightly skewed angle, making the man in the picture seem to tilt like the Leaning Tower of Pisa.

I didn't remember that particular photo session. It was one of hundreds in my childhood, especially in my teen years when the house really began to rock. By then, I was running out of space. Scenes crowded the surface of the house, impressionism rubbing elbows with realism, realism back-to-back with abstract expressionism. The house reflected me, my moods, the mile-a-minute changes going on inside my teenage mind. It seemed I changed styles weekly. And so, the house changed too.

I smiled at the photo and thought of cameras and Papa. My father loved cameras but was a photography klutz. When people asked him to take their picture, he fumbled with the cameras, searching for the right buttons. He would frown and scratch his head and someone would offer to help. But he would say, no, he'd figure it out. He loved to tinker. Then came the day he worked his first Polaroid. When the film rolled out of the camera like a tongue, he almost jumped out of his overalls. He watched the picture materialize with incredulity. He asked if he could do it again. That one looked a bit off center, he said. He thought he could do better. Thereafter, he was always a bit disappointed when folks shoved an Instamatic or thirty-five millimeter camera in his hand. They could have given him the world's most expensive Leica and he would have looked at it with chagrin. Papa was hooked on Polaroid.

George hated living in a point of interest. He was lousy at PR. At first he was proud of the house: "I never thought I'd live inside a Niagara Falls or a Lincoln Memorial." For a while he even enjoyed talking to "our tourists." But soon he grew bored with the Clydes and Sallys from Missouri and the Moniques and Todds from Manhattan. It got to the point where he ran in the opposite direction when someone even said the word "camera." Finally, George shot his own photograph of the house, printed it up on postcards, and displayed the postcards next to a locked, slotted box on the porch. On the box was a sign:

POSTCARDS 50 CENTS
HONOR SYSTEM
NO NEED TO RING THE BELL
WE TRUST YOU

During my George period, as Wynn the art expert calls it, the house took a turn for the worse. I wasn't painting like I once did. The painting I did while living with George somehow didn't seem to fit the house. The house stopped changing. Scenes began to fade. Fewer people came. And then George made that lethal suggestion at the dinner table: the Whitewash Proposal. When the pictures were gone, no one was interested in pulling out their Polaroids.

My father never owned a camera. It never occurred to him to buy one. I captured all the likenesses around our house—on our house. I realize now we should have bought a camera. We never planned for the future, for the contingency of meeting a man named George who had a fondness for white paint and a disregard for dreams. I sniffed, wiped the back of my nose with my hurt hand, and cursed at the pain.

"Are you all right?" Thomas asked, glancing nervously at me.

"Medication," I lied. "It works like a sad movie on me." I pointed to the picture. "You look like him," I said. The man in the photograph was Thomas's father. Thomas, too, had blonde hair. Not as long as the man in the photograph but just as sun streaked and thick. Thomas's hair was short and spiky. He had a body that, as Freda would say, looks good in jeans. The license plate on his van was issued by the state of California. He had a smile you expected to see all over San Diego, a surfer's smile, teeth white as foam and Hollywood straight. How did they get teeth like that? I wondered. It must be all the fresh fruit they eat.

"What's your last name?" I asked.

"Mellon," he said. It figures.

I have always had the worst teeth. Just looking at a piece of chocolate cake could make them crumble. Dr. Willard, my dentist, said decay could find my mouth blindfolded. Thomas smiled at me. I squinted into those bright, plastic-perfect teeth. He was all of the great age of nineteen. I was married at nineteen. I'd lived a whole life since then. We had nothing in common. He was just beginning.

Thomas was skipping college that semester. Sure, his parents were disappointed, but they understood. I didn't. From what I could make out, Thomas was traveling as his father, the man in the picture, had: to find himself. It was an old-fashioned sixties thing to do in a time when business schools were murdering the other disciplines. It seemed everyone in the world wanted to learn about accounts receivable. Except Thomas. He didn't know what he wanted to do with his life. "What do you like to do?" I asked.

"I enjoy looking at the stars," he said.

That led me to the obvious career choices—shepherd and

astronaut. Thomas said he'd tried Space Camp when he was in high school but found the whole experience "too technical." Now shepherd was something he hadn't considered. "I'll give it some thought," he said.

In the meantime, he planned to continue his search. He drove the same vehicle, a yellow Volkswagen van, that his father had steered more than twenty years ago. It was not keen on exploring America with another yearning, searching, stoned cowboy. It demanded new tires in Denver, a fan belt in Kansas City, a quart of oil in Ohio. It threw a fit until someone cleaned its spark plugs in Boston.

I am familiar with the temperament of vans. T-Bone and I found my olive eyesore in a field five years ago. It was decorating some guy's back forty. The moment I flung open the doors I knew I wanted it. The insides had been gutted. It was a great green metal shell. My footsteps echoed as I climbed in and paced off the distance from end to end. The owner said he could get it running, and even threw in a passenger seat, scrounged from the adjacent pasture, for free. What a bargain, I said to T-Bone.

What a mess, George said. He wanted to know how T-Bone could let me buy such a thing. T-Bone said he kind of liked it. George fumed. I smiled and T-Bone smiled. The van started pinging three days later and hasn't stopped since. I listen to the talk shows on the radio where drivers call in with questions about their cars. From those shows, you'd think America was one big automotive anomaly, full of cars that you'd rather put up with than give up. That's the way I feel about my van. Mechanics from all over the world could look at my van—the way it pings on uphills some days and downhills others, how it starts on cold mornings without a hitch but won't even roll over on warm summer days that seem like a Bahamas vacation—and not figure it out. But I don't care.

We drove Thomas's van to the doctor. I hunched in the back, out of sight, amid a sleeping bag, a huge backpack, a cardboard box of books and cassette tapes, a pair of binoculars, several posters of stars and celestial systems taped to the wall, two dumbbells, a computer, and a half bushel of apples.

The doctor pronounced Thomas fit despite his queasiness, but insisted on putting nine stitches in my palm. I was afraid of that. I hate needles—hypodermic, sewing, knitting. The last time I had to be stitched up was when I was seven. Odie Dorfmann was the king and I was about to be his new knight. He lifted the snow shovel to tap my shoulder, missed, and knighted my head. Ten stitches and a new hairdo. My father was frantic, turned to Jell-O by my tears and the sight of blood pouring down my face. He held me all night, rocking in the rocking chair, watching over me as I slept off the painkillers. My hand pulsed with pain. Suddenly I was sad that there was no one to hold me that night.

When we pulled in the drive, I saw T-Bone waiting for us, tilling the front yard with his nervous feet. He rushed to the van as Thomas parked, pulled my door open, and helped me out.

"Why didn't you call me?" he said, walking me toward the house. Thomas followed us. "I walked right into the house—you've got to start locking your door, Maud, anyone could walk in. I found the blood upstairs and nearly went out of my mind. Your van was here but you weren't. I called Odie, Freda, Wynn, even Reverend Swan. He suggested the doctor. The nurse said you were already on the way home. She said you're all right. Are you?"

"Thomas drove me to the doctor after we wrapped my hand up so he couldn't see it."

"I never could stand blood," Thomas smiled.

"The doctor said Thomas would be fine as long as he stayed away from automobile accidents, wars, and sharp knives."

"Sound advice," T-Bone said, his arms crossed over his chest now.

"Even after my hand was wrapped, Thomas made me sit in the back of the van. He wasn't taking any chances. He didn't look in his rearview mirror once the whole way."

"So much for defensive driving," Thomas said sheepishly.

T-Bone turned white. I knew what T-Bone was thinking: that Thomas could have killed us both, could have pulled out to pass when the guy behind him already was passing; that, from the looks of the van, he'd been in a few wrecks; and that he probably didn't even have a license.

"Show T-Bone your license," I told Thomas, leading them into the house. I headed for the refrigerator. Thomas complied with a big white smile and T-Bone frowned.

"You're growling," I said, passing T-Bone a beer. He took it and downed half in a gulp.

"You should have called me."

"T-Bone, nine stitches, for gawdsake! It was nothing."

"Did the doctor give you a tetanus shot?"

"Yes, dear T-Bone." I turned to Thomas. "T-Bone worries about me."

Thomas smiled. "He's a good friend."

Eventually, after two beers, T-Bone began to relax. We talked of other things, the weather and vans and apples. Thomas said he bought the bushel in the back of the van at a roadside stand. Apples for breakfast, lunch, and dinner. When he was a child, he said, his father told him he could brush his teeth by eating apples. But only on camping trips.

It was growing dark when T-Bone stood to leave. He looked pointedly at Thomas. I told Thomas he was welcome to stay the night. He accepted the invitation with a flash of teeth. T-Bone grunted.

Without comment, he walked outside. I left Thomas nursing a soda at the kitchen table. T-Bone's hands were shoved in his pockets and his head was turtle-sunken into his jacket. We waded through the leaves to his truck. At the truck, he faced me.

"Are you going to be all right? Did the doctor give you some painkillers?" I nodded. "Eat some supper, OK? Promise." I promised and he sighed. I touched his arm.

"You know there isn't a motel room to be found this time of year," I said. "They're probably already putting up people in the National Guard Armory. It's only for one night."

"I know."

I watched him out of sight. I stood in the twilight, trying to see him clearly, long after he'd gone. Finally, I noticed the night chill and my throbbing palm. I turned back toward the house and Thomas.

6

The Crime Wave Begins

The day went down in Odie Dorfmann's casebook as the beginning. The note read in the typically dramatic style of the books he reads: *Someone is stealing Round Corners's art.*

If it smacked too much of Sam Spade or Philip Marlowe, you had to remember that Odie the lawman sees everything through the grimy pane of crime. His nose constantly sniffs for the smell of gunpowder. His ears are perpetually perked, like a cat's, for the sound of the hammer of a gun being stealthily cocked behind him. Except for when he's building birdhouses, he hardly ever relaxes.

Odie was on the alert that morning, sitting beside me on my porch step, scraping the label off an old beer bottle. (Odie wouldn't think of drinking on duty.) He snapped the bubble gum in his mouth. Odie is a longtime bubble gum fan, probably something to do with all those baseball cards he used to buy. When he quit smoking last year, he became a certifiable addict. Giving up cigarettes had been George's idea. When he died, George was pestering Odie to launch a regular running program.

Odie's visit was one of many by my friends and neighbors. My farm had become the Grand Central Station of Round Corners. People dropped in night and day. They interrupted meals. When they didn't come in person, they telephoned. And they all had the same thing on their minds: the painting.

"It's a virtual campaign," said Thomas, who was still bunking on the couch in his sleeping bag. In a week, he'd taken over the cooking and the laundry. Ella and Wynn think he's cute. Rever-

end Swan wants to know how long Thomas intends to stay.
T-Bone just growls at him. And Sheriff Odie Dorfmann, protec-
tor of the innocent and artists who don't know better, doesn't
trust him.

"You can't take in everyone who comes to the door, Maud,"
Odie said, attacking the beer label with his thumbnail.

"I took in George," I said, watching Thomas. Across the yard,
he raked leaves into one pile after another, pushed the piles
together, then whisked them onto an old blanket. When the
blanket became full, he dragged it to the road and dumped the
contents on a bigger pile, a mountain of leaves as high as a
snowdrift, ready to burn.

The autumn sun was deliciously warm if you were relaxing on
a porch trying to ignore nosy public servants, but plumb hot if
you were bullying around thousands of leaves. Thomas flung his
flannel shirt on a bush. Underneath the shirt he wore a grey
T-shirt with the words "Rock Is on a Roll" printed on the front.
Underneath the T-shirt were young, healthy muscles. They were
not as massive and well defined as T-Bone's muscles, nor as
sculpted as George's.

Odie glared from Thomas's back to the shirt on the bush.
"That was different."

"How? George just showed up at my door one day, too. Just
like Thomas."

"George was a man, not a boy. He liked baseball. He was a
veteran, for chrissake."

"And he didn't like rock 'n' roll."

Thomas leaned on the rake, smiled at us, and waved. Odie
harrumphed and blew a bubble. I waved back.

Odie freely admits there are some people he just doesn't
understand. I am one of them. He can't comprehend why I
refuse to paint the mural. Artists, he says with disgust, are always
waiting for the muse. "Ordinary people can't afford the luxury of
a muse," Odie says. "Do you think I wait for the muse to chase
down tax evaders, rapists, and murderers?" Those were Odie's
priorities. In some ways, he was very much like George.

Thomas raked under the maple, banging his head on a bird-house made by Odie. The dangling aviary swung and twirled. Odie chomped on his gum, probably doing irreparable damage to his bridgework. "That kid probably doesn't know one end of a purple martin from another," Odie growled.

When Odie wasn't capturing criminals or pitching shutouts for the Round Corners Royals, he built birdhouses. Simple birdhouses for robins and complex birdhouses for cardinals. Apartments and condominiums for communal birds such as the purple martins. Sometimes, when he was in the mood to run the jigsaw, he decorated them with gingerbread and Victorian curlicues. Odie's wife, Arlene, shakes her head when he gets carried away. Like the time, during the Reagan administration, when he built a birdhouse that was the exact replica of the White House.

I don't think Odie goes off the deep end with the bird accom-modations, but then I didn't think anything about painting a huge Andy Warhol/Campbell's soup can on the side of the refrigerator either. I think Odie would go a little cuckoo without his birdhouses. No one wants a repeat of the winter of '89 when Odie broke three fingers arresting an unruly drunk. In the tussle and heat of apprehension, Odie slammed his hand in the door of the squad car. For six weeks, life was hell in Round Corners. A frustrated, bored Odie set up license checkpoints and speed traps. It took forever to get anywhere.

At the moment, Odie was building a miniature Swiss chalet, similar to a home built on the other side of the mountain by a Wall Street executive. It had the feeling of a hideaway about it, Odie said. The idea for the hideaway birdhouse came to him in the middle of the night. He woke up one morning and knew exactly what to do. The way he described it, it sounded like a kind of muse, but Odie doesn't believe in muses.

Odie believes in birdhouses, baseball, and America, in that order. Odie, a scared eighteen-year-old grunt, arrived in Vietnam in the fall of '73. Twelve weeks earlier he had been strutting down the halls of Round Corners High School, making crude jokes with his football buddies. Nothing had prepared him for Vietnam. Years later he and George would sit watching a war movie in our living room and shake their heads at the cinematic fiction; war was nothing like television, they said. Odie may have hated Vietnam, but he loved the army, he loved the idea of "serving."

The concept of serving, that Odie so wholeheartedly bought into in the army, laid the foundation for Odie the sheriff and town selectman. He was proud of his job and sincerely loved the town and the people in his care. Also, it didn't hurt that he was built to be a lawman. His appearance lent itself to the illusion of intimidation. Just about everyone—except the schoolchildren who met him on Career Day—knew if it didn't concern the flag, birdhouses, or baseball, Odie was seldom riled.

Odie was never out of earshot of an AM radio. He worshipped baseball and the AstroTurf on which it was played. Baseball was sacrosanct to Odie Dorfmann, politician, lawman, creator of homes for birds, most valuable player of the Round Corners Royals (1979–81). So it was understandable why Odie almost had a heart attack the summer of '92. He had to sit and listen to all his favorite teams slide, while a Canadian upstart clawed its way to The Playoffs. "Do you know what this means?" he asked his wife Arlene. "Do you have any idea what this could do to baseball? My God," he said, "Canadians in the World Series." Arlene said she hoped the Canadians won; that would shake things up. "You don't know what you're talking about," Odie said.

Arlene got her wish. The Toronto Blue Jays won the 1992 World Series, sending Odie into a two-day funk. He retreated to his workshop and could be heard hammering and sawing long into the night. On the third day, he emerged with a scraggly beard, a new birdhouse, and a smile. Those birdhouses have saved Odie's health, mind, and marriage many times.

To tell you the truth, I never had much patience with Odie until one evening when I overheard him talking with George. He was reminiscing about his childhood (the kind of stuff no one's ever interested in) and he said something, described a sound that I wished I had heard.

"I love to hear the crack of the bat," Odie said.

Apparently, to hear the kiss of ball and bat through the static of the radio was all it took to put Odie over the fence into the dreamland of his childhood, to a time when everything was baseball gloves and statistics. Name a record, and he'd tell you the fellow who made it and the guy likely to break it. If you were looking for a certain baseball card, all the kids used to say, you went to Odie; he had a regular vault under his bed, until his mother made him clean his room. Yogi, Roger, Mickey. He knew them all and someday, he dreamed, they would know him.

"Someday," he told his mother, "I'm going to hit a ball out of this world. Plop. Did you see that? It landed in a crater on the moon." "Eat your cereal, Odie," his mother said.

Odie told George what it would feel like to hit that ball. "I will know it's the one the moment I connect. Its greatness will reverberate down my arm. I'll feel it in my muscles; it's impossible not to feel something that smooth. I'll stand for a moment and watch it, contemplate the ball I sent to the stars, then I'll skip once, twice, and head for first. I'll take it easy, a token run for the crowds, but still the bases will disappear under my feet like the steps of an escalator. And when the reporters grab me and ask how it felt, I'll just say, 'It was heaven, boys, heaven.'"

Odie divulged to few people the rest of the dream. There was a feeling, he said, that always came over him at the end, just as the ball was almost out of sight, a feeling that it didn't matter who had hit that ball, that it was headed for the universe at that particular moment in time, and he just happened to be the guy who gave it a lift.

"Sometimes when I build birdhouses," Odie told George that night in a whispery voice, "I get the same feeling, that I'm an instrument, a channel. It's not a helpless feeling, not an out-of-control feeling," he said, and here I had to practically put a glass to the wall and lean my ear against it to catch Odie's words, "because I seem to be not only the tool, but the person using the tool." Silence. "Weird, huh?"

I called to Thomas, "Take a rest."

He mounted the porch. "You watch, they'll multiply while I'm gone," he said with a grin, then entered the house.

"I don't trust people who smile that much," Odie muttered.

I laughed and shouted to Thomas to bring another beer with him when he came.

Odie chewed his gum. "About this painting, Maud . . ."

"No."

"Now don't go getting on your artistic high horse."

"I mean it."

"Think of the greater good."

"Forget it."

"This artistic stubbornness does not become you. George would want you to do this, you know he would."

"George was a stinker."

"There's no talking to you when you get like this." Disrespectful, he meant. "I ought to lock you in a cell with some paint and throw away the key."

I offered my wrists to Odie.

"You know, Maud, you're awfully cocky for a former shoplifter."

I gasped and dropped my hands.

"Maybe I ought to run you in. You can think about the errors of your ways and my painting, too."

"How'd you find out?"

Odie shifted. He studied the toes of his boots. "George had too many Rolling Rocks one night. The Expos were whipping the Bosox. You know how he loved the Bosox. It just sort of slipped out. He was mad at you about something or other and we got to talking . . ."

"George told you," I said faintly.

"Maud . . ."

"He promised he would never tell anyone."

Odie blew a bubble, a dinky one, hardly worth puckering for.

"Look, forget I ever said anything, OK? We've got to concentrate on this painting . . ."

The CB radio in Odie's official sheriff's car crackled and buzzed. Odie ignored it until it spewed the voice of screeching Wisconsin Dell Addleberry across the yard.

"Calling Sheriff Dorfmann. Calling Sheriff Dorfmann. BM, you got your ears on?"

Odie cursed and lifted himself off the step with a groan. "Someday I'm going to strangle that woman. With the cord of a CB radio." Dell was his dispatcher.

"Sheriff Dorfmann. BM, you out there?"

Odie swore, grabbed the microphone, and shouted at his dispatcher. "I told you not to call me that!"

"Sheriff, is that you?"

"Goddamn, Dell, of course it's me."

"Please identify yourself with the proper badge number. This *is* official police business. We can't give out this information to just anyone, you know."

Odie struggled to control himself. His hands shook. He opened one fist and discovered he had crushed a tiny birdhouse shutter he'd found in his pocket.

Wisconsin Dell, conceived in the resort of her namesake of parents who never saw each other after that weekend, was born with a stutter. She was raised by New England grandparents who never encouraged her to talk for fun, much less profit. I don't know how she landed the job of police dispatcher. But I know she'd never leave it.

When Dell first came to work for the sheriff's department, Odie gave her a manual of police codes. She loved the official-ness of the book, the state seal on the cover, the idea of talking in some secret language. But, most of all, she loved all the syllables the codes saved. Dell figured she saved thousands of sounds a year. That was important for someone who considered speech her enemy.

The only problem was Dell couldn't remember the codes. She studied the book day and night. And still, when time came to relay crucial information, her brain went blank.

When it became obvious that his new dispatcher would never master the manual, Odie decided codes weren't that important.

Of course they were, said Dell.

So Dell made up her own. BM was Boss Man in Dell's private codebook.

"Please give me your authorized badge number. That is if you are the *real* BM."

Odie began to speak slowly through gritted teeth. "I'll give you numbers. Take this number down. Three, seven, zero, nine. Form three, seven, zero, nine. That is a form for dismissal, and, if you don't start talking to me, you can just get one of those forms out of the filing cabinet and fill it in with your name. In triplicate. As in the number three. Fired, fired, fired."

There was a pause on the airwaves.

"You plan to work on one of those beautiful birdhouses today, Sheriff?"

Odie sighed and shook his head. "What's up, Dell?"

"B and E. Breaking and Entering."

It was early for people to be breaking into camps. Vandalizing vacation homes was the usual form of crime in Round Corners—bored kids or cold transients who pried open a window to the summer place of a stockbroker from New York or a stockbroker from New Jersey or a stockbroker from Boston. They prowled around, ate the food that had been left behind, smoked any cigarettes they found. Sometimes they slept there. Sometimes they took a radio or an electric can opener. They never did the dishes before they left. The drunk who smashed Odie's fingers in the car door was a bum who'd jimmied open a cabinet of Grand Marnier in a camp on Pine Tree Road.

This call, however, wasn't someone's camp.

"Wynn Winchester says someone stole her knitting needles—her lucky needles."

"Dell, is this some kind of joke?"

Even across the yard, I could hear Dell bristle over the airwaves. Nothing about the law or Dell's part in its maintenance was humorous to Odie's dispatcher.

"I do not joke about the big B and E, BM."

When Odie investigated the report, he found that the thief had walked past a color television, a videocassette recorder, a new exercise bike, and a silver tea set belonging to Harvey Winchester's great-great-grandmother—all to get to Wynn's knitting basket near the woodstove. The needles Wynn used to make all those sweaters for Harvey, the needles that were to knit the clothes for her precious unborn child, were last seen in that basket.

7

Living with an Electronic Mailman

Of course, given my criminal past, I was the first person George suspected.

I may have been a petty shoplifter at one time, but I was never a knitting needle thief, George. Besides, I'm reformed. And Wynn is my friend. And I hate needles.

It's true, George, she's been bugging me, almost as much as Odie, about this mural thing, but I wouldn't steal her lucky knitting needles. It's too terrible to even consider. Everyone knows what those needles mean to Wynn. She's so superstitious about this pregnancy that if someone held those needles for ransom, she'd clean out her bank account without giving it a second thought.

Not even for spite. I am not spiteful, George.

I didn't put your underwear in with the navy blue sheets to get even with you after you called one of my paintings antediluvian. It was a mistake. Jesus, George, haven't you ever made a mistake? What do you mean, no?

I was looking up antediluvian in the dictionary when I put the underwear and sheets in, and they just got mixed up. I wasn't paying attention. That's all.

Navy blue underwear is very sexy, George.

I wondered what color underwear T-Bone buys.

Freda and I hitched up our skirts and flopped into the empty booth like two fish. She lit a cigarette, sighing at the taste of nicotine. I wiggled my toes. The service station attendant across the street closed up for the night, cutting the lights in the station and over the old pumps, locking the door. He left illuminated the big Exxon sign floating in the sky.

"I'm worried about Wynn," Freda said.

"I've never seen her like this."

"I was in the shop yesterday, and she was just sitting under one of the hair dryers staring off into space. It was running full blast. And this was *after* she'd styled her hair."

"Harvey doesn't know how to handle her. He's spending more and more time at work. I don't understand it. He loves her so much, and he's so excited about this baby."

"Lewis Lee says he's afraid." Freda shifted and her polyester whispered. "Lewis Lee says most men don't know what to do with pregnant women; it's all those hormones raging about."

"I wish there was something I could do."

"Wynn's just lost without her knitting."

"She says she's tried other needles, but everything gets full of knots. Muddled somehow."

"It's all mental."

"Isn't everything?"

Two tall sodas sweated between us. Each had a straw. Freda's straw was branded with the imprint of her Sensuous Midnight red lipstick. I lifted the soda with the clean straw to my lips and filled my taste buds with Mountain Dew. "So what do you get mental about?"

Freda smiled. "I get mental over Lewis Lee in our big brass bed."

I shook my head and laughed. "All you ever think about is Lewis Lee and sex . . ." I stopped and stared out the dark windows at our reflection, Freda so content and happy and fulfilled, me so confused and empty and full of unrest. I quickly glanced away.

Freda crushed the cigarette tip in the ashtray and lit another. The smell of burning sulfur wafted across the table. "So," she said. "Tell me about the kid."

I thought about Thomas, waiting at home, probably reading one of his astronomy books. He refused to go to sleep until I came in. Some nights, when my feet were heavy from walking the meals marathon at the Round Corners Restaurant, Thomas massaged them. His fingers are gentle like starlight. They are unerring in their hunt for aching joints and muscles, relentless in their pursuit of the fallen arch. They perform with certainty, like a comet on a predestined course, and I've begun to look forward to the night when the stars come out and Thomas's fingers wait for me.

"He's cute," Freda said.

"He's nineteen," I said.

"Lewis Lee is a year younger than me. Most people don't know that. Younger men make a woman feel frisky. You should try it."

I shook my head. "I don't understand him. He's got everything: money, looks; I think he's probably a genius. And he just drops out of school so he can loaf. I told him he was screwing up his entire timetable. He'll have a hell of a time making his first million by the age of thirty at this rate. But he just laughs at me."

"So he's a smart kid."

"He's a smart-ass." I ran my hand through my hair, dislodging it from the braid. "I thought everybody wanted to go to college these days, to learn to make money."

"You said he has money."

"His parents do."

"Same thing."

"You know, his parents don't even have indoor plumbing." Thomas told me half the week his mother and father lived simple lives without electric can openers, microwave ovens, or take-out pizza. The other half they worked with, talked with, played with some of the most sophisticated computer hardware in the country. They were high technologists. They ran computers that ran corporations.

"They like working with high technology but hate living with it," I explained to Freda. "Ten other families live on a piece of land with them. They're all friends from their hippie days."

Freda perked up. "Like a commune?"

I shrugged. "Apparently, they went to college together and were in the peace movement together. His mother grows all her own food, organic, you know, no fertilizers, and his father chops wood to keep the house warm. The house isn't much bigger than a trailer. When they plug all the computers in, they blow a fuse."

"A commune, as in free love, free sex?"

"Will you forget about Lewis Lee for one minute? Three times a week, Thomas's parents throw on their corporate duds and drive to Silicon Valley to work. They're very good at their jobs. You can't get away with living the way they do if you're not. The company psychologist says they're going back to the earth, seeking to renew their relationship with nature, because high technology has made them feel alienated and isolated. Thomas's mother says she just likes fresh vegetables." Freda and I exchanged glances. "No plumbing," I said.

"And a house full of computers," Freda said, shaking her head. "Well, I think you ought to consider the situation. You could use some romance in your life, some free love, some no-strings sex. You've been irritable lately."

"It's that damn painting everyone keeps talking about."

"Men are wonderful inventions."

"Haven't you heard? Women don't need men to be complete."

"Who says you have to need them? Just enjoy them. I'm not saying it would be the great love affair of all time; Lewis Lee and I have that distinction. But it would improve your disposition."

"I'm not irritable."

"You're horny."

"He's a child! He writes home every week. He has a portable computer in the van that he hooks up to my phone and sends letters to his parents. He calls it electronic mail."

Freda nodded toward the post office down the street. "For gawdsake, don't tell Ella about that."

The next week Odie made three visits to my house nagging me

about the painting.

"No," I said. "You can throw me in jail, feed me bread and water, make me watch old videos of World Series games. But I'm still not doing the painting." Odie mumbled something about using blackmail when he had the chance.

Odie was getting nowhere in the investigation of the missing knitting needles.

On Friday, Wynn spiked Mrs. Weaver the librarian's blue hair. Mrs. Weaver screamed when she looked in the mirror. Wynn tried to calm her: "The punk look is *très chic* right now, Mrs. Weaver."

"But I look like the bride of Frankenstein."

"Not many women can carry that look. You've got the bone structure to handle it. And it couldn't be more timely with Halloween around the corner."

Mrs. Weaver began to cry. She was somewhat pacified, however, when Wynn announced that the cut was free. Of course, it was a mistake like George's underwear and the blue sheets. But it tore Wynn apart. Professional pride, she said. She hadn't done something that boneheaded since beauty school. And besides, she said, she couldn't afford to keep giving her work away.

As Freda says, "There is nothing sadder than a beautician run amok." I remembered all the times Wynn had looked after me: how she kept me from looking like a scarecrow in the school pictures (Wynn was always ready with brush and hair spray in the girls' bathroom) and how she talked me out of the black leather wedding dress. Throughout my life, Wynn had always understood how hard it was for me to function in a world not of my making, in a world without my house and paints. Wynn understood that some things—such as how to dress and act at a prom—never entered my mind. While other girls thought in terms of Friday night dates and new pink ski pants and teen magazines, I was immersed in Matisse and mauve paint and the way you can draw a guitar with a few strokes of the brush. I knew nothing about girl things, and Wynn knew everything. As Papa used to say when faced with one of those embarrassing adolescent girl questions, "Thank God for Wynn."

I thought of all the times Wynn had saved me (even when rescuing wasn't all that important to me) and asked Wynn if she would do me a small favor: pose for a few sketches. "Sketches," I told her sternly. "This has nothing to do with the Round Corners painting, so don't get up your hopes."

"Oh, yes, please, Maud," Wynn gushed, drying her tears on the hem of her maternity smock.

I patted her arm and sighed. I never could stand to see Wynn depressed. So I'm painting again.

I don't have any intention of doing the Round Corners mural, George; it's just a painting. It could be any old painting. It doesn't have to be of Round Corners.

I don't know what it's going to be, but whatever it is, it's four months pregnant.

8

Fred Astaire with a Limp

Every morning Thomas drives into Round Corners and buys the *New York Times* at Snowden's General Store. He reads the newspaper to me, his leg dangling over the back of the sofa in the studio. Current events are a compulsion with him. It probably has something to do with being raised by "ists": activists, pacifists, environmentalists, humanists, high technologists. Apparently, his parents served politics at breakfast with the wheat germ, fiber, and nuts. Harvey Winchester says all the baby books encourage talking to children from the moment their blurry eyes blink upon this world. In fact, it's almost negligent not to yak at them in their car seats, at the dinner table, during diaper changes. I'm sure Thomas's parents read the same book, but I bet they didn't discuss the color of a maple leaf or a cat's soft fur. "My parents care so deeply about so much, Maud," Thomas said. "Sometimes they make me feel as if I don't believe in anything at all." Forget the cat; Thomas cut his teeth on conservation, women's rights, environmentalism.

As Thomas read aloud, his voice alternated between good humor and outrage. Unlike T-Bone, who read the newspaper anesthetized by a tap-dancing high, Thomas had no protection from anger induced by corruption, horror generated by injustice, pain produced by stories of South African children maimed by rubber bullets. Thomas is the type to hear the children's screams a globe away. He has that kind of sensitivity, so strong it's almost touchable, so appealing it almost overwhelms a woman. The sun poured in the window in the roof, splashing over Thomas, turning his yellow hair golden. I thought, he doesn't fit in this studio with its uncaring white walls.

I laid down my pencil with a trembling hand and got a beer.

"You shouldn't drink beer this early in the morning, Maud," lectured Wynn Winchester, nestled in a rocker brought up from the living room. According to Wynn, this was the universal pose of mothers-to-be—swaying in rockers, patting their stomachs. The Madonna with Bloated Belly look.

I placed the beer can on the table with restraint.

Wynn chattered, "I've given up all alcoholic beverages, drugs, and cigarettes."

"You never smoked cigarettes," I said.

"Not after that time in the cemetery. Jesus, I thought I was going to die. Remember we stole a pack of Marlboro cigarettes from Daddy's dresser and sneaked out to the graveyard? We scrunched behind the headstones and puffed until we were sick."

"How old were you?" Thomas asked, lowering the newspaper.

"Children. Just kids. Twelve, I think."

"Tell me some more. I want to know everything about Maud. Was she cute as a kid?"

"Not as cute as me," Wynn said. "I always had to style her hair. She never even combed it for school pictures. She couldn't be bothered. All she thought about was her art."

"Sit still, Wynn," I said.

"I am sitting still."

"Your lips are moving. Thomas, read us another story."

Wynn said Thomas had a melodious voice, even when reading of mayhem. His tongue did not stumble over datelines such as Reykjavik. He read story after story, so poised, so witty, so grammatically correct. At last, he finished the paper, tossed it on the floor, and folded his arms across his chest. "We ought to be doing more about the homeless," pronounced Thomas.

"I'm doing my bit," I said. "I took you in."

"I mean in a political sense. We could go sleep in boxes in front of the White House." I ignored Thomas. "We could protest. I've never been in jail, but Mom and Dad have been arrested tons of times." He studied the skeleton branches of the trees through the skylight. "Now they express their political views with their bucks instead of their bodies. They unloaded all their stocks in South African companies long ago. They have a 'socially responsible' investment counselor. What did George think of socially responsible investing?"

George thought it was a crock. "Who knows who's dumping what in the dead of night?" George used to say. That was one of the things I trusted about George: He didn't trust anybody.

I concentrated on Wynn's hair. She wanted to be a brunette in the painting.

Thomas the philosopher persisted. "It's tough to know what to believe in, y'know. I mean nothing's for sure. You think you're doing one thing and end up doing something else. Like the soldiers in Somalia. They just went there to feed people—to keep kids from starving—and now the people they were trying to help want to kill them. It's crazy."

Wynn snorted. "Well, I tell you what I believe in: babies." She patted her protruding abdomen.

I smiled. "I believe in washing my belly button once a week."

Thomas laughed. "I believe in hamburgers with as much fat and grease as you can squeeze in them—real cholesterol monsters."

Wynn made a face. You could turn her green with just the word "bacon."

Thomas, who enjoyed exasperating and/or shocking Wynn, went on, "Of course, being a Californian, I also believe in real estate, which is not to be confused with the environment. Oh, and the big one, The Earthquake."

Wynn shuddered. She was not a fan of geological disturbances. Wynn the mother-to-be liked to feel the earth firmly under her feet. When she walked, she slid her feet forward in a searching way and cradled her swelling stomach, ever on the lookout for a gopher hole or a tree root waiting to trip a pregnant woman.

Thomas and I exchanged grins. It was impossible not to like

the kid. He had the ability to fit, like a puzzle piece, even in a
town of strangers. In a few short weeks, Thomas had become
a part of Round Corners. Everyone, but T-Bone, liked him.
T-Bone called Thomas "Spaceman."

"I'm into exploring space," Thomas once told T-Bone. "The
one out there." He motioned to the sky. "And the one in here."
He tapped his forehead.

Thomas liked to ponder those stupid meaning-of-life ques-
tions. What is happiness? Does it make sense of your life?
Where do you find faith? On a mountain? At church? In a
painting? What is art, and what is life?

"What else do you believe in, Maud?" Thomas asked.

I saluted them with my Rolling Rock. "I believe in country-and-
western music."

Wynn left in a rush. "I've got women waiting for me at the shop,
probably swinging from the hair dryers in anxiety. All the fe-
males in Round Corners want to look pretty for carving the bird."
Thanksgiving was a week away. "Thomas, are you going home
for Thanksgiving?"

"My family doesn't eat meat," Thomas said.

"It figures," Wynn muttered, grabbing her purse and hustling
out the door.

"Watch out for the gopher holes on the stairs," I called, giving
the sketches one last glance before heading for the kitchen.

Fortified with another beer, I set out to prepare dinner. In less
than an hour, the kitchen table and counters were covered with
no fewer than twelve cookbooks, all opened flat and speckled
with flour, gravy, and grease. All the cookbooks were borrowed
from the library, a habit I got into while living with George. I
always checked out art books for me and cookbooks for George.
If the blue-haired librarian could see her books now, her hair
would probably turn back to its original white color.

In the past week, since Wynn had been modeling for me, I
had renewed my resolution to learn to cook. I made chicken
tetrazzini, leek soup, beef bourguignon, Szechuan duck, and

cheeseburgers—none of which resembled the pictures in the books.

George often told me anyone could cook, if they wanted to. He had been doing it for most of his adult life and didn't understand how I could find it so difficult. Cooking only required attention. Or so he said. "You must care for your cuisine as if it were a Cassatt," he said. George was an impressionist chef.

"Attention!" George admonished, pointing his finger in the air like the French chef of a five-star restaurant or a Nazi commandant. "You can't cook a meal properly and doodle on a tablet by the stove at the same time." Once my sketchpad caught on fire. George put out the blaze with a pot of French onion soup. I cried for two hours—over the sketches, not the soup.

I read the recipe again. Garlic powder. I spun the spice turntable. Garlic salt, but no garlic powder. I reached for a different cookbook, one with a conversion table. It showed how to convert garlic powder into garlic salt but not garlic salt into garlic powder. Damn, I needed George. George loved to figure the correct measurements and proportions. He doubled and tripled recipes just for the mathematics. Forget the garlic powder. I opened a can of tuna. The smell of sea washed up my nostrils. I held my nose and dumped the tuna into the macaroni and cheddar. The recipe didn't say whether or not to drain the tuna. What was the correct consistency of tuna casserole?

Upstairs Thomas flipped on the shower. I listened to the water rushing to Thomas, rattling pipes all over the house on its way. I didn't want to come to care for Thomas. He could be as persistent as George was, as single-minded, too. He was mixed-up and searching and cute. I didn't want to like him, or worry about him, or begin to ask his opinion. And I didn't want him fixing my roof.

Just a week ago, I was telling Amos and Bartholomew about Thomas's bent for home maintenance. "Roof, eh?" said Amos, with a frown. "Tricky things—roofs."

"Have to have toes like a fly," said Bartholomew.

"I've seen men who have worked in construction all their lives catch a boot tip on a loose shingle and slip right off the edge."

"Good way to break a leg," Bartholomew nodded.

"Leg! Hell, a twenty-foot drop'll kill you. Break your neck, if you land just right. Snap it like an icicle," Amos said.

"That's a fact," said Bartholomew.

During a lull in business that afternoon, I dashed home, sure I would find Thomas dead by the porch. Taking corners on two bald tires, twisting the van's steering wheel like a stunt driver, I wondered about notifying his parents on that little computer and worried that I wouldn't remember how to use it. But when I pulled my old green van in beside his yellow one, he was straddling the roof, grinning. He waved a half-empty soda bottle at me and asked why I was home early.

"I'm not!" I screamed at him. "And don't drink on the roof." I slammed back into the van and drove slowly back to the restaurant, steering the van with trembling hands.

I focused again on the tuna casserole. That was a week ago. Thomas was still absorbed in the roof project. He seemed to have a sixth sense about hammers and nails and two-by-fours. What he couldn't figure out he asked about—on one of the on-line computer services. He simply logged on to a bulletin board devoted to home repair and posed a problem. Within twenty-four hours, he had a dozen suggestions for approaching it. It was better than the Time-Life Books, he said.

Someone tapped at the back door. I waved T-Bone in, smiled, headed for the refrigerator, and took out two beers. I handed him one. T-Bone glanced at the disaster area of pots, pans, food, and books. He cautiously approached the dish on the stove.

"Tuna casserole," I said. T-Bone's eyebrows jerked.

"Still can't figure out how to paint that damn mural, huh?"

I edged him aside with my hip and shoved the casserole into the oven. I slammed the door with expert indifference and stuck my nose into the air. After a moment, T-Bone said, "Heat would be good here." I turned on the oven.

We took our beers to the table and sat. He told me about one of his sick cows, about a song he'd heard on the radio, about the new birds visiting his bird feeder. I leaned my cheek on my hand and listened. T-Bone has always talked of these things with me, and I've never grown bored. His voice is soft, and it has a slight accent. Wynn says she can listen to an Englishman talk all day. I feel that way about T-Bone. But he never would—talk all day—so I have to catch every syllable I can, when I can.

He motioned toward the window and the roofing materials outside on the grass. "What are you going to do when he finishes it?"

"God, I don't know," I sighed. "I'm hoping he gets bored before it's done."

"Not much chance of that. I think Spaceman's here to stay."

I slipped my hand across the table and touched T-Bone's arm. "He's a nice guy."

"What does he do besides piddle with the roof?"

"He works on his computer, and he studies the stars. Every night he stands in the front yard, staring at the sky through his telescope. Sometimes, I think he stays out there all night."

"It'll be cold soon."

I shrugged. Thomas wandered in, barechested, barefooted, his blonde hair wet from the shower, his jeans clinging low on his hips. He smelled of shampoo and soap. He greeted T-Bone and opened a soda from the refrigerator. He leaned against the counter and downed half the bottle, then casually pushed aside a Vietnamese cookbook, four eggshells, a shoe, and a hammer, and hopped up on the counter. His bare feet dangled in the air, his toes wiggling.

Thomas asked T-Bone what he thought of the homeless situation. T-Bone said it was a sad thing in a country as rich as ours. Somewhere music was playing, rock 'n' roll, switched on by Thomas after his shower. The singer said he wanted sex. Thomas tapped his fingers to a beat I could barely hear.

"I'm trying to talk Maud into going to D.C. with me to protest our government's indifference to the homeless," Thomas said. "We could sleep in boxes in front of the White House."

T-Bone's long, lovely fingers tightened on the beer can. "She could be arrested."

"That's the point."

"She could be hurt." T-Bone crumbled the beer can in his fist.

"You said yourself the homeless situation wasn't right."

"She could catch cold." T-Bone looked at me.

"Don't worry. I'm not going today." I smiled at him. "Today I'm cooking tuna casserole."

T-Bone nodded and rose, gripping my shoulder for a moment as if it were aluminum instead of bone. "I've got some time on my hands. I'll split some wood for you."

"Thomas already has," I said.

T-Bone stared at the young man with the pearly smile then searched my face. "I better get back to the farm then," T-Bone said.

"But I appreciate the offer," I said. "Why don't you come back for tuna casserole?"

Thomas jumped off the counter and stood by me. He flung a friendly arm around my shoulder. T-Bone studied Thomas's arm as if he were contemplating amputation. "Wouldn't miss it."

But he did.

The remains of that horrid tuna casserole were in the waste-basket, drying up and turning brown, when T-Bone called.

"Where are you?" I demanded.

"It must have been one helluva casserole," T-Bone said.

"You wouldn't know, would you? You chickened out."

"Maud."

"George hated it when people didn't at least try everything on their plate. If they didn't show up at all, they were off the guest list forever."

"Maud."

"What?"

"Can you come and get me at the hospital? They've shot me full of drugs, and they won't let me drive."

"Hospital? Drugs?"

That afternoon, as T-Bone chopped his own wood for the winter, the ax slipped and cut off two toes, two of his dancing toes. I yelled at Thomas the whole way to the hospital, as we bounced and swayed down Highway 100 at eighty-five miles per hour.

"He said he wasn't watching what he was doing. How can you not pay attention swinging an ax as long as your arm? How can you miss a whole fucking chopping block?"

"He's going to be OK, Maud."

"Why didn't he call me?"

"He did."

"He should have called sooner."

9

Going Eight Rounds
on the Top of Machu Picchu

The night was quiet and full of waiting. My father would have
said he smelled snow on the cold night breath. For the moment it
was clear, and Thomas was in the front yard with his telescope.
He was searching the skies, as usual.

He shouted, calling me. I pulled on a coat and ran outside.

"I think I saw it," he laughed. "It was just a smudge of light in
the sky, but I know it was a comet."

It was a cold sky, perfect for a speeding snowball. Thomas
huddled in his down vest. He had forgotten his gloves again. I
returned to the house, found his gloves, and took them to him.

"Here, put these on." Thomas absently pulled on the gloves.

"I did see it," he cried, grabbing my hand.

I studied the sky. It looked as if it had dropped thousands of
feet and we could reach up and pluck a star. It was coldest when
it was this clear. The day's warmth escaped and mixed with the
heat of the stars making them twinkle even brighter.

"Did you know that sunlight and solar winds always keep a
comet's tail pointing away from the sun?" Thomas chattered.
"When Halley's Comet left the solar system in 1986, it sped
away tail first like a family movie played backward. When it
returns, I'll be eighty-eight."

"And I'll be one of those stars in the sky," I said, "just a smudge
on the cosmos."

He burbled on about comets and how people used to think of
them alternately as the souls of heroes on the way to heaven and
the messengers of disease and doom. "How could anyone be
afraid of a comet? How could anyone be afraid of anything in the

heavens? It's so beautiful up there."

"We're not afraid of comets," I said. "We love them." I remembered Amos and Bartholomew wearing Halley's Comet
T-shirts and how Freda's son begged for a Halley's Comet cap
for Christmas. "That mail-order house is selling those caps for
fifteen dollars a pop," Freda said with disgust. "And they're ugly.
Nothing but a baseball cap with a comet streaking through the
crown."

"Everyone wants to know about comets," Thomas said. "Will
they shed light on our beginnings? Do they hold 'the stuff of life,'
as scientists believe?" Thomas laughed. "My father was about
the only one who wasn't excited about Halley's. He said, 'You—
man—hold the stuff of life.'"

"You don't believe him?"

"Sure. Some days."

I left Thomas hunting the skies for comets and went to bed.
Since Thomas was making himself at home on the sofa, I had
moved back into my room. I slept badly in the pale room. I
snuggled the covers up under my chin and thought of T-Bone's
room, how dark and cozy and simple it seemed. T-Bone chose
wallpaper with deep hunter green and burgundy, earth tones.
It's a warren of a room, like the office, a hole where a man can
hunker down amid his farm magazines and cologne-smelling
sheets. It's a solid room, a room that holds you and that you can
hold on to. It is nothing like my room, like my entire house. All
the walls in my house are white, and the furniture is furniture
color. For such a realistic decor, nothing seems real here. I hate
my room the most. It lacks substance, heart; it has the soul of a
turnip. It fills me with dreams.

George is always in them, of course, wearing his softball
uniform. He stands in the center of the attic studio, his hands on
his hips, popping gum. He rocks back and forth on the heels of
his baseball shoes and asks what I'm doing.

I am painting.

George shrugs and starts pitching a ball up in the air, tossing it
over his head, pretending it's a high fly ball. He dodges in front

of the painting to catch it. "Lucky you still paint those little greeting cards at the Round Corners Restaurant," he says, diving for the ball and crashing into the canvas. He grabs the canvas, rights it, and retrieves his ball. Again and again he tosses the ball, each catch leading to further destruction, each bobble ending in overturned jars of brushes, smashed chairs, and squirted tubes of paint. Finally, when the studio is sufficiently wrecked, he heads for the door.

I closed my eyes.

What I wouldn't give for one night's sleep, a peaceful sleep, maybe dreaming of bulls. Powerful Picasso bulls.

The cows were bawling when I pulled into T-Bone's yard the next morning. It was ten o'clock. Clouds had rolled in while I was wishing for dream bulls. The weatherman predicted snow by nightfall. I slapped my cold arms and believed him.

Inside the barn, everything was quiet except an orchestra of angry cows. They wanted to be milked, and they wanted the deed done now. I flipped on the radio as I passed through the milk room. The cows shuffled uncomfortably in their stalls. I tried to soothe them as I began hooking up the machines. I spoke to them in what little French I knew.

"T-Bone knows I hate this beaucoup," I told one put-upon bovine. "I bet he overslept on purpose, just to spite me. I try to help him around here, and I don't get an ounce of appreciation, not one *merci*."

A cat, one of the huge extended feline family that made its home in the barn (no relation to Cat on the couch), rubbed against me. I shook my finger at it. "The human you own is a very poor patient. I've met bears with better dispositions. You have to wrestle him to get him to eat. And his diet stinks. Beer and potato chips. Potato chips and beer. I try to get him to eat a pretzel once in a while, just for variety."

I patted one cud-chewing bossy and shoved her to the side to reach the milking machine. She looked at me with sympathy in her eyes. "He sleeps on the couch in the office. In his clothes.

His conversation's gone to hell. Doesn't read the newspaper anymore. He even forgets to fill the bird feeders. Speaking of food, would you prefer the hay à la orange or the hay cordon bleu today? Don't worry; I didn't cook it."

When I finished with the cows, I stomped into T-Bone's house, knocking the barn from my Nikes on the doorjamb. I tossed my coat on a hook on the wall, washed my hands, and took a six-pack from the refrigerator. I knew where to find him.

T-Bone's bandaged foot was propped up on the coffee table, which was covered with empty beer bottles, empty beer cans, and empty bags of potato chips. Crutches peeped out from under the sofa. Cat slept on his chest. He rolled on his side and groaned; the last edge of the afghan slipped to the floor.

The temperature in T-Bone's office was freezing. I built up the fire in the woodstove. Then I scooped up some birdseed from the bag in the corner and ran out to the bird feeder. The wind was coming up and blasted its way through my sweater. I slammed the door loudly on my way back in.

"You don't have to make all that noise. I know I forgot the birds."

"And the cows."

"And the cows." T-Bone sighed, rubbed his unshaven face, and focused on me with bleary eyes. He shoved himself to a sitting position, dislodging the cat. Cat leapt to the table, knocking over several beer bottles, then to an old leather wing-backed chair, her chair.

I passed T-Bone a Rolling Rock. He twisted the cap off and tossed it on the floor. I opened my beer, lifted the cat, and placed her on my lap. T-Bone said I was the only one who could do that—separate Cat from chair—without losing an arm. The birdhouse outside the window was vacant, the residents packed and moved south for the winter. The bird feeder, however, was still doing a brisk business. Winter birds were like skiers: always hungry. Cat, perched in my lap and watching the birds, licked her chops.

I motioned toward the cat. "Does she need food, too?"

"She takes care of herself."

I sighed.

"Don't look at me like that, Maud."

"Like what?"

His eyes dared me to pity him. My glance skittered away, jumping from T-Bone's books to his desk and computer to the bird feeder outside.

"You know, when I got the call from the hospital and they told me George was dead, I went up to the studio and drew a cow. A fucking cow. I spent hours on that cow getting it just right."

"You never did."

"Nope."

"It could have had something to do with the number of legs."

"You think because you're a dairy farmer you're so smart. *That* was an abstract cow."

"I don't feel like arguing art with you, Maud." T-Bone sighed. His beautiful body was propped against the couch like a cane against the wall. He seemed stiff and uncomfortable under my gaze. There was no music playing in the house, yet his good foot tapped the air. He crushed the beer can with one hand and motioned for another. I tossed one to him. He caught it, kicking the crutches further under the sofa with his tapping foot.

In a few weeks, the doctor said, T-Bone could look forward to a cane. T-Bone took the news with the good humor of a rattle-snake caught in a trap.

"I heard you cut off your whole leg," I said.

"Bet I know where you got that information."

"Amos and Bartholomew," I nodded and swallowed. The beer stung the back of my throat. "If the politicians pass another safety law, Amos and Bartholomew will blame you." I recalled the debate over T-Bone's disability.

Bartholomew said, "I heard T-Bone chopped off his big toe."

"Naw," said Amos, "it was the whole foot."

"It was a *very* big toe," insisted Bartholomew.

"Those boys in Montpelier get wind of this and we'll be wearing steel-pointed boots," said Amos. "It was incidents just like this that led to that damn law requiring us to wear those damn things on our heads."

"Earphones," Bartholomew said.

"Earphones," Amos said with disgust.

"That's a fact," Bartholomew said.

"Two toes." T-Bone lifted his beer in a mock toast. "It could have been worse."

I shrugged. "As Amos and Bartholomew will tell you."

We sat in silence. The wood settled and snapped in the stove. Afternoon came and grew darker. I broke open another six-pack, as well as potato chips, pretzels, and corn chips.

T-Bone shook his head. "You can keep the Doritos."

Cat jumped from my lap and patted at the plastic six-pack rings piling up by my chair. I popped the top on another beer, spraying her. She took refuge behind the stove. I leaned my head against the back of the chair.

"I read some conservation group is sending volunteers to clean up the trash on the mountaintops," I said. "They hauled tons of garbage—tents, stoves, oxygen tanks, cans, food wrappers, clothing, six-pack rings—off of Everest. Can you believe it?"

"Sure."

"Remember when we used to go hiking? You always were a stickler about trash. I'd come off the mountain with my pockets full of papers and cans."

"I sold the cans to the recycling center. Paid for our gas."

"Why did we stop doing that?"

"You married George."

"That's right."

I sighed and cradled my beer bottle. "Now, people spend their vacations scrounging for diet soda cans on the Alps and granola bar wrappers in the Machu Picchu ruins of Peru. I wonder what Machu Picchu is like. Let's go and see. When your foot gets better, we'll take a sanitation vacation. We'll pack our hiking boots and collect high-altitude garbage for a week."

"I've never taken a vacation."

"You'll be in heaven."

T-Bone finished off the potato chips. He rubbed his eyes.

"How about if I fix us some real food?" I asked.

"You and what cordon bleu cavalry?"

"You need something else in your stomach besides a bunch of worthless calories."

"Don't worry about my calories."

"Someone's got to."

"You know I never knew this before, but you can be a real nag, Maud."

"Who do you think I learned it from?"

T-Bone groaned, lifted himself up from the sofa, and hobbled to the bathroom. He avoided using the crutches whenever possible, whenever there were plenty of available walls and doorjambs to catch himself on and plenty of time in which to get where he was going. I jumped up from my chair to help. He glared at me. Finally, he turned and I stuck out my tongue. While he was in the bathroom, I pulled the shoelaces from my Nikes and tied his crutches together. He returned and carefully levered himself back on the couch.

He studied me and frowned. "Well, I'm not going to worry about you anymore. You look prettier than I've ever seen you."

"Thanks, that's a really rotten thing to say." I leaned over him. "Don't you want to know if I'm sleeping at night?"

"No."

"Don't you want to know if I'm working too hard?"

"No."

"Don't you want to know about the painting?"

"No."

That did it. I strode to the kitchen, grabbed my coat from the hook, and shoved my arms through the sleeves. I stalked back into T-Bone's office. "For your information, I can't sleep worth a damn in that god-awful pale bedroom. I'm working like a dog. And the painting is shitty. The colors are all wrong. The animals don't have the right number of legs, and all the people look pregnant."

"I don't want to know!"

"Fine."

"Fine."

I turned to leave, then stopped and gave him a sweet smile. "Oh, and by the way, Thomas will be over in the morning to help you milk the cows."

"I don't want him on my goddamn property." T-Bone struggled to his feet. He rummaged under the sofa for the crutches. "I'm warning you, Maud, you tell that kid if he comes on my land, I'll shoot him on sight."

"You don't own a gun." I headed for the kitchen. I could hear T-Bone struggling with the crutches. He knocked the cans off the coffee table and cursed. "Maud, what have you done to my crutches? Come back here, Maud!" T-Bone bellowed. "I own an ax . . . and a chain saw. I'll saw that kid in half. After I saw these damn shoelaces."

"You'd probably miss him, considering your current accuracy with sharp implements."

"Maud!"

"He's only going to help."

"I don't need his goddamn help."

"Well, you're getting it anyway. Because I don't like cows."

T-Bone screamed. "Goddamn, Maud!"

As I slammed through the back door, I heard T-Bone yell, "That goddamn van is pinging again. Have the kid listen to it. Before it breaks down on you somewhere."

"What do you care?"

"Do it, Maud."

Thomas could call up the automotive encyclopedia on his computer, get some idea of what the problem was. T-Bone was not mechanically inclined. He was not inclined toward anything anymore—a situation I personally was familiar with but had never identified with T-Bone.

I took the road home slowly. The mile between T-Bone's and my place had never seemed so long. The road was empty. Waiting. I passed my drive, carefully reversed, and turned. I parked the van sideways, climbed out, and approached the faded painting of Milky Way. Suddenly the Rolling Rocks and my argument with T-Bone got to me. I was so tired. My legs gave out and I decided to sit. That's where Thomas found me when he came out for his nightly sky watching, asleep on the cold ground. He lifted me into his arms and carried me into the house. I opened my eyes and smiled at him.

"You're a funny kid. Do you have any information in that computer of yours on Machu Picchu?"

10

Mailwomen Have Elephant Memories

Country-and-western music poured out of the radio in the studio. The theme was lovesickness, as usual. I thought of T-Bone. He was milking the cows again. Thomas's presence had a stimulating effect on him, as I knew it would.

"I go to work in the middle of the night," he warned Thomas that first morning.

"So do astronomers," smiled Thomas.

To his surprise, Thomas liked working with the cows. He'd never had much experience with anything bigger than a dog before, anything that stepped on your feet one minute and licked the hat off your head the next. He was accustomed to animals whose shit fit in a pooper-scooper. He said he was learning valuable things. He had given up the life of a protester and was now leaning toward the Peace Corps.

Thomas explained the intricacies of a milking machine to anyone who would listen. Today it was Wynn, as she trimmed his hair by the sink in my studio. An old paint rag was draped around his shoulders like a beautician's cape. It was pinned at the neck with a clothespin. I watched Wynn snip at Thomas's blond hair and wondered if she was doing her pelvic squeezes.

Wynn said she could do twenty pelvic squeezes while she was curling Marie LeBeau's hair. Marie, a schoolteacher, had short, black hair. She liked the curl tight, close to her head. Every time she came in, she said to Wynn, "Give me a do those kids can't undo." Marie taught ninth grade English. (She told every new group of kids, "Please don't tell me about your love lives in the first personal essay. Give me something to look forward to.")

Wynn said the squeezes went like this: She wrapped a strand of Marie's hair around the hot curling rod, held it for a moment just as she held her pelvic muscles, then released both her bottom and Marie's curl.

Wynn purchased a book that gave instructions for all kinds of exercises for pregnant women. She performed her exercises daily. Whenever she had the chance, she squeezed, lifted, or tightened something. The book said if she did the exercises faithfully, her delivery would be easier, and she would regain her shape more quickly after the baby was born. Harvey said he couldn't understand it: First, she couldn't wait to get fat enough for maternity smocks, and now she was worried that she'd need them for life. Wynn told Harvey he knew nothing about prenatal care.

"This will fall right in shape for you," Wynn told Thomas as she combed and clipped. "No fuss. No muss."

"Just right for my busy lifestyle," Thomas said.

I dabbed sienna on the canvas. I finished sketching Wynn shortly after Thanksgiving, yet she continued to stop by more days than not. The smell of paint no longer affected her like a rocking boat; she and the baby were cruising through the second trimester. She seemed more contented here than at the shop. She always brought something to eat, a cake, a pot of chili, a casserole. I tried to ignore the chocolate chip cookies on the table.

Wynn told Thomas, "I have known Maud all her life—did she tell you we were in geography together?—so I know about creative urges. They are special things. You can't just shut them off when you want to. They possess you. It's a craziness in you. You wait and see. Maud'll forget to eat and sleep and change her shirt. She'll come into the Round Corners Restaurant looking deader than yesterday's meat loaf. It used to drive George nuts. We've got to take care of her."

Thomas said he would.

"I couldn't do what Maud does," said Wynn, tilting Thomas's head forward to clip the little hairs along his neck.

The phone rang. I concentrated on the sienna and ignored the phone. Thomas started to get up, but Wynn shoved him back in his seat.

"Maud, will you get that, please?" Wynn said. "We're busy here."

I wiped my hands on a cloth and grabbed the paint-speckled telephone. It was Ella Snowden. She didn't even say hello, just launched into some story about losing the notebook in which she was writing the poem to go with the mural. It was to be the epic saga of Round Corners and its residents. She'd searched the house, the car, the entire post office.

"It's not like me to misplace anything, no matter what Frank says, and especially not a notebook. Frank says I'm the most disorganized woman in Round Corners, and if I lost one of my notebooks, it was my own fault and no reason to take it out on him." Ella sniffed. "It's amazing how you can be married to a person half your life, and they still know so little about you. You don't get to be an employee of the United States Postal Service by losing things."

Ella has been writing poetry for forty years. She has never been published. The closest she ever comes are the little rhymes she writes at the bottom of her Christmas cards. The people of Round Corners like Ella Snowden's "verses"; some even admit they look forward to them Christmas after Christmas.

Each year Ella took one week of paid vacation from the United States Postal Service and attended a writers conference in Middlebury. Also, each year Frank tried to talk her out of it. "I miss you too durn much," he said. But Ella wouldn't give up those seven days for a chance to meet John Keats, Emily Dickinson, and Robert Frost at the same cocktail party. Now, if you threw in Allen Ginsberg, she might be tempted. "That Ginsberg fellow is somethin'," Ella says.

At the writers conference, Ella pretended she was not an old woman running a rural postal route, threatened every year by budget cuts. She mixed with the young people and listened to their ideas and loaded her notebooks with thoughts. And she wrote poetry entirely unlike the poetry she penned in Round Corners.

Conference poetry was about politics and loneliness, about war and fear, about the land and love. She wrote all night at the conference. She wrote while miles away Frank snored and dreamed. In the morning, the young students found her asleep, bent over a notebook on the table, her grey hair wild from scraping fingers. They hesitated about waking her but knew she would be upset if they didn't.

So they woke her. They watched her struggle up from deep dreams, heard her whisper "Frank," and then her eyes would pop open, awake and more alert than her young colleagues. They helped her out of the chair. She grew stiff during the night and often needed to lean for a moment on one of the young men. Someone would hand her the notebook. She would smile and thank them as they entered the dining room.

"The dining room," Ella says, "is always buzzing and clacking and banging. It's not the food trays you're hearing; it's the words. They fly like a gaggle of geese over your head, honking, drawing your attention, making you smile at the joy of life. I'm so contented in that dining room."

I'm one of the few in Round Corners privileged to read Ella's conference poetry, and Ella said the Round Corners poem was like those. "I didn't intend it to be so, but the words are spilling out of me, Maud. In buckets. It frightens Frank; hell, it frightens me."

This passion poetry, Ella said, seemed out of place in Round Corners. For one thing, she could not pull all-nighters in Round Corners; she tended to give people the wrong mail when she had less than eight hours of shut eye. And this time of year—the Christmas season—she especially needed her wits about her.

This poem was different in other ways, too. It did not rhyme. All her Round Corners poetry rhymed. This poem just seemed to grow. It was born in a tumult of words tumbling to the paper, a waterfall of words. Sometimes it was a swampy mess, and other times it was a miracle. Ella had never before had a poem come to her in this manner, where she felt more recorder than writer.

"Is this the way it was with you and the house, Maud?" she asked.

I knew what Ella was experiencing: the joy of the smooth ride. There was nothing like being possessed, to be driven and to drive. We come back again and again to feel that feeling one more time. We're creativity druggies, and we'll do anything to find that high again. We'll put up with recalcitrant cows and dead husbands who still think they know more about art than we do. I have tried everything to find my way back: Rolling Rock, perseverance, meditation.

Nothing works.

As my farmer father used to say, "It comes when it comes." I envied Ella.

"Is this the way it is with Ginsberg, Maud?" Ella asked me one day. "All this fury? All this joy? All this inevitability?"

Frank did not like Ginsberg. He did not want Ella reading Ginsberg in bed at night. He said it was silly to read something you didn't understand. But Ella could not resist Ginsberg's words; they rattled around in her head, filling it to bursting, until it no longer mattered that she didn't know what a "peyote" was. She told Frank poetry doesn't have to rhyme all the time, and wasn't "angelheaded hipsters" a lovely image? Frank huffed.

Ella named her poem about Round Corners "Howling Mad Home." Allen Ginsberg wasn't the only one who knew crazy people, Ella said.

"Have you looked in the stamp drawer?" I asked her. "How about the mailbags? Maybe it got mixed up and found its way to Montpelier."

Ella gasped. "Oh, that can't be, it just can't be."

"Take it easy, Ella."

"But, Maud, if that notebook should fall into the wrong hands . . ."

"We're not talking government secrets here, are we, Ella?"

"I write everything in my notebooks. Things I don't even remember writing in the first place, thoughts I never knew I thought. 'Howling Mad Home' was not a cat poem; it wasn't a rhyme about spring or a daffodil verse. It was about real people living and loving, people who took out the trash and scratched their bellies. If the contents of that notebook ever became public, I would have some explaining to do, Maud. There are references to certain friends, certain neighbors, *a certain husband*."

I tried to soothe Ella. She and Frank were married forty years ago. It was a small ceremony in a little Catholic church up the mountain. They started attending Reverend Swan's service when the diocese turned the chapel in the mountains into a resort. Neither she nor Frank skied. They never had children. Up in the closet she still had a box of napkins engraved with golden wedding bells and "Ella and Frank." How's that for hanging onto something?

Ella said she knew Frank better than she knew herself. She could tell from the look in his eye whether he wanted hotcakes or Quaker Oats for breakfast. She knew he was afraid of heights and hated putting on the storm windows each fall and taking them off in the spring. She knew, at that very moment, he was probably sneaking a nap in the rocker by the woodstove in the store next door. Because she knew him so well, she figured he probably hadn't meant it that morning when he said she would forget her head if it wasn't attached.

"When was the last time I lost something of his?" Ella cried. "I have accounted for forty years of socks, underwear, handkerchiefs, tools, and receipts."

"I'm sure he'll apologize tonight," I said.

But he didn't.

I helped Ella look for the notebook, but it was as if it just vanished, disappeared into dust. Wynn said she bet it was the knitting needle thief. "Don't be ridiculous," Harvey Winchester said, which is not unusual since Harvey couldn't agree with anyone lately. Thomas drove into Burlington one morning and returned with a new notebook for Ella, a lovely hardcover book with blank pages and a gingham print cover. Wynn gave Ella a new perm in my sink, to pull her out of her funk.

"It's a perfect perm, not too tight," I said, smiling at Ella. Her bottom lip quivered as she stared at her reflection in the mirror.

"Just right, Mrs. Snowden," Thomas agreed.

"It's you, Ella," Wynn said.

Ella sighed.

I sighed.

The next day I found myself sketching Ella. She held a quill pen in her hand and wore a lacy, high-collared blouse. She sat at an angle and looked off into the distance. Below the soft blouse she wore blue pants with dark stripes down the side, part of the official ensemble of the United States Postal Service. Ella wanted only to be pictured from the waist up. She thought her hips were too big. I sketched her full frame, and when it came time to draw the blue linen uniform my pencil made the shape of billowing skirts, flowing, romantic, unofficial.

Wynn, leaning over me as I worked, gripped my shoulder happily.

"It's the spitting image of you, Ella," she said.

"Haven't you got some pelvic squeezes to do?" I growled.

11

When a Snowflake Is Not As Light As a Feather

The van gave out halfway up the mountain. The Olive Eyesore said, "Ciao, baby." The Artmobile said, "See you around the old Seurat." The Cause of One of My Great Fights with George threw in the towel.

This was not your normal breakdown. This was a Stranded Motorist in the Dead of Winter breakdown. The cold snap turned into a full-fledged winter—and a way of life—three days ago when it began snowing. Snow continued to fall, sticking like an unwanted houseguest.

Motorists dared not let their gasoline tanks get low in case they met up with a whiteout, steered into a tree, and had to cool their heels until help arrived. They were especially wary if they drove a beast vehicle, like mine, which has a mind of its own. I tapped the fuel gauge; it *said* half full. George said he wouldn't believe that instrument of faulty information if it swore on the Bible.

That's the difference between you and me, George. You expect all machinery to lie to you. I prefer to think of it as one of our mechanical friends showing a little creativity.

No, George, creativity never killed anyone, except maybe an airplane inventor or two. I know I could freeze to death; thanks for reminding me.

The engine only uttered its last cough a few moments ago and already my toes were frostbitten. I realize that is medically impossible. The van still had some stored warmth. I wasn't exposed to the elements, except for the wind that whipped through the cracks around the windows. They have never rolled up completely. I've preferred it that way; usually it gives the van that wide-open-spaces feeling. But when you're wondering about the human capacity for withstanding subzero temperatures, you begin to see the advantages of tight windows and doors.

I have been stranded before by my mercurial mechanical amigo. Experience kept me from going into hysterics and ripping up the upholstery for dinner.

I don't have to worry about food, George. Someone will come along. Check the glove compartment for candy bars? Don't be ridiculous.

I plunged into the glove compartment. There was an opened package of stale rye-and-cheddar crackers and three sticks of gum.

I thought I had a can of Pringles in there. Why would T-Bone steal my potato chips, George? He wasn't always mooching off us. I invited him to dinner because I wanted him around. He was a great conversationalist, and he always helped with the dishes. We talked of other things, besides cows. Name them? There was . . .

I know you never trusted him; he never trusted you. So what's new? The men in my life never trust each other.

I popped a stick of gum in my mouth. The taste of cinnamon flooded my taste buds, making me hungry. That's the way it is when you're stranded: All you can think about is food and warmth. It doesn't matter if you just finished a seven-course meal that a small Third World country could live off of for a week. It doesn't make a bit of difference that you're wearing three wool sweaters; a down parka that explorers tested against the blizzards on Mount Everest; insulated, top-of-the-line, straight from the L.L. Bean catalog boots; two pairs of gloves, one silk and the other lamb's wool and leather; and a hat that better be warm because it makes you look ridiculous. You're still hungry and cold, from the moment the engine goes kaput.

I climbed between the seats and dug around in the back of the van. I unearthed an old army blanket under a shovel and three empty paint cans. I wrapped the blanket around my shoulders and crawled back into the driver's seat.

Isn't this the way it always happens, George? I've started painting again, nothing earth-shattering yet, but it keeps that buzzard sheriff from the door. Wynn and Ella are preening like mother hens. No one has asked to see the painting yet. They're afraid they'll destroy the muse. They just hover and cook and offer to run errands for me. I'm painting, and now I'm going to lose all ten fingers to frostbite.

I closed my eyes and leaned my head against the seat. At that very moment, T-Bone was probably curled up with a Rolling Rock and a bag of chips by the woodstove. Cat was probably chasing a potato chip across the floor. Maybe I could send him a psychic call for help. According to Raj, we're all connected by one mother of a consciousness.

Tap, tap. Tap, tap. I jerked awake. It worked; T-Bone found me. I swung toward the tapping at the window and screamed. Pressed against the window was a face from hell, fat lips moving like fish mouths, eyes crossed, nose squashed into a Picasso proboscis. I collapsed against the seat. It was Odie.

"Gotcha, Maud," Odie laughed.

"You moron," I clutched my heart.

I don't care what Raj says, there is no way that Odie Dorf-mann is tuned into the collective consciousness. You have to be a member of the food chain to join that club. So it was pure luck that my Volkswagen Vixen broke down on Odie's beat.

Odie had two more stops on his daily rounds. I waited in the patrol car as Odie rattled the doorknob on the summer camp. He checked the windows and peered inside, his gloved hands cupped around his face. Odie made his rounds whether the mercury shot to ninety or plummeted to nine.

"I wouldn't mind a week on the beach," Odie said, blowing on his fingers and bundling into the police cruiser. "The only things on television lately are basketball and travel ads. 'Come to our island. Lie on our sand. Eat our fruit. Drink our Mai Tais.' Hell, I don't even know what a Mai Tai tastes like."

"It has a little umbrella in it."

"No shit?"

I nodded. "To keep the cherries and orange slices from getting sunburned."

The closest Odie was likely to ever get to a Mai Tai was in one of the Chinese restaurants in Burlington, according to Odie's wife, Arlene, the lifetime spouse of a public servant and keeper of the checkbook in the Dorfmann household. A public servant's budget didn't stretch to islands and exotic-sounding drinks with umbrellas. Nor did the sheriff's heart.

Arlene and the rest of the town knew that for all his talk of tropical paradise, Odie felt responsible for Round Corners and its people, especially in winter. He could not thaw out in the Bahamas while his friends remained frozen fish sticks in Vermont. He had to look out for people like me.

Actually, Odie is probably a good lawman. He takes a personal interest in the people he's sworn to protect. And he has to be one of the most honest politicians in the whole United States. He has no illusions of grandeur; he's fairly incorruptible. He doesn't have his eye on a higher office. He isn't greedy, and he has an almost boyishly innocent respect for the law. He simply likes being the biggest frog in our little pond. If he ever lost an election, it would hurt his feelings more than anger him.

Running unopposed most of the time, Odie has little chance of not being a selectman, yet he still persists with campaign promises and posters. In Odie's tiny mind, they are part of the democratic system, even if they are superfluous. Odie is like the bidder at an auction who keeps bidding against himself.

"I'll send one of the boys from the service station for your van, Maud," Odie said, reaching for the police radio.

"Don't bother," I said. Tomorrow Thomas would drive me out to the Traitor Vehicle and it would turn over with one try. It would purr like one of those babied autos at the Indianapolis 500. I'd been the victim of this automotive contrariness before.

Odie didn't understand people who left life to chance or put up with menopausal mobiles. He regularly checked on the old people in town, just to make sure chance hadn't played a dirty trick on them and held up their emergency fuel funds. He didn't want any frozen bodies in his county, Odie said, pretending to be tough: It wouldn't look good. Last year, the Dorfmanns ran short of wood for their own stove because softhearted Odie had snitched repeatedly from the pile. Just taking a "few sticks" over to so-and-so to tide him over until his wood's delivered, he told Arlene. She nodded. She'd heard it all before.

Odie taxied motorists to service stations, called for tow trucks, carried booster cables in his trunk. Wisconsin Dell Addleberry's car was dead more than alive. She always needed a ride to work. He told her she ought to scrap that pile of junk. She said it worked fine in summer. Summer? he said. Vermont had no summer. It had winter and Fourth of July, a small patriotic thaw about the size of a melting Popsicle. If it had any summer, it was Indian summer. This was no place for Wisconsin Dell's Florida Ford.

Odie stopped in and said hello to Old Ed on Mountaintop Road. You need anything? he asked. No, Old Ed said, staying close to the stove. Odie loaded his big arms with firewood at Old Ed's woodpile, carried the wood in, and stacked it neatly by Old Ed's stove.

Coming down the mountain, Odie switched on the radio. *They lost their minds today,* Odie sang with the Everly Brothers. *They threw their love away. They act as if they were born yesterday.* Odie would not have lasted two seconds in a barbershop quartet. As he sang, his head bobbed and his fingers tapped. The rest of him, squeezed into the squad car, was immobile. He was bundled up to about the size of a polar bear, a heavy coat buttoned over his huge chest.

Odie rocked on until he came to Beaver Creek Road. Just passing the snowy avenue made him growl. The sign was gone again. But that was not the real reason Odie lost the beat of the song. I live on Beaver Creek Road, and I'm still holding out for a reprieve on the painting. The last time he nagged me about it, I slammed the door in his face. I told him I'd have it done by Town

Meeting, good-bye. Bang. Almost broke his nose.

Odie shook his head and chewed his gum. "Artists are the most absurd people on this earth. No offense, Maud. But we pamper the artists in this country. All those grants we give them, and look what they do with the money—they create pornography. They can't handle life like the rest of us. They're soft. Thank God they don't run the country."

"Oh, I don't know, Odie, it seems to me . . ."

Wisconsin Dell Addleberry's voice screamed at us over the police radio, interrupting the Everly Brothers.

"Calling car four-zero-niner. Four-zero-niner come in, please."

"Four-zero-niner—I mean, Sheriff Dorfmann here."

"Good afternoon, BM. I got an SM—Stranded Motorist—on Highway 100 two miles out of town. Called it in himself on his car phone."

"This is the day for the automotive unlucky. Call him back, and tell him I'll be there right after I drop Maud off at the restaurant."

Pause. Odie and I heard the sound of papers being shuffled. Dell cleared her throat. I saw Odie brace himself. Dell did not put off things. She functioned on the principle that you might as well take the medicine and get it over with. Whenever Dell stalled, it did not bode well for Odie. He chewed faster.

"What is it, Dell?" Odie coaxed.

"I've got another B and E."

"Ah, shit."

"BS ain't all you're going to say, BM."

"Give me the location, Dell."

"The B and E was reported at Thirteen Snowflake."
Silence.

"BM, are you there? BM, answer me. Omigod, I think he C and B'ed—Crash and Burned. BM? BM!"

"Would you repeat that address, Dell?"

"Thirteen Snowflake."

"That's my house, Dell."

"Yes, sir, your wife just called it in."

Odie stepped on the gas and we bobsledded down the mountain, taking the curves sideways, using the snowbanks to keep us from flying off into the pine trees.

Sheriff Odie Dorfmann wandered around the remains of his garage in a daze. He picked up a screwdriver and laid it down. He hunkered before the little electric space heater he used when the weather turned cold, flipped it on, saw the coils begin to redden, and flipped it off. He lifted a tiny chimney into the air, squinted his eye at it, and returned it to the table. His wife said she never heard of a birdhouse with a chimney.

"I'd planned to build a tiny woodpile on the porch of the house. I figured it would make a nice perch," Odie said.

The old roof of Odie's garage had collapsed under the weight of the recent snowfall, crushing Odie's birdhouses like an avalanche. Apparently, Dell had been trying to say BD, Birdhouse Disaster, instead of B and E, Breaking and Entering, but just got her abbreviations confused in the gravity of the moment. Dell, more than anyone else, understood the scope of this catastrophe. Odie was devastated. The man who had created a whole other city above Round Corners, a tiny town in the sky, a winged village, was lost.

Odie stepped over shattered bird-size A-frames, ranch houses, and antebellum plantation mansions. He stood at the window, his shoulders hunched, watching the birds fight at the feeder. Snow fluttered down on his head through the missing roof.

"The cardinals like the sunflower seeds. Sunflower seeds are more expensive, but I think the cardinals are worth it. They're a baseball bird. I love baseball birds: cardinal, oriole, blue jay. Well, not so much the jays, they're pesky. Precocious, really."

A blue jay dive-bombed the feeder scattering titmice and sparrows everywhere. "Just like they horned in on the World Series. Who would have ever thought a Canadian team would win the greatest of American games? Absurd. The Communists probably put them up to it."

A woodpecker rapped in the pines. Odie smiled sadly. "I left that one dead pine there just so the old boy had something to bang his head against. Arlene's terrified that dead tree is going to fall on the house one night in the middle of an ice storm. Wives can be absurd."

I exchanged a glance with Arlene. She shrugged and blew her nose in a wadded tissue.

"I took the top off that tree long ago. If it did fall, the most it would get was a corner of the back bedroom, the one Arlene's mother sleeps in when she visits."

Suddenly Odie picked up a bucket of softballs and a bat from the corner of the garage. He rested the bat on his shoulder and waded through the deep snow in the backyard. When he reached the middle of the yard, he dropped the bucket of balls and hefted the bat. He hit a ball, then another; ball followed ball. Like a lonely boy popping pebbles into a lake with a stick, each time he tried to hit the ball farther. It was easier to measure distance in the snow than it was in a lake. The balls plopped, sinking two or three feet in some cases. Impressions in the snow represented singles, doubles, triples, home runs.

Eventually, there were so many impressions, they became muddled. Balls were lost. I stood in the doorway of the ruins of the garage and watched Odie swing the bat again and again. He should have painted orange stripes on the balls, I thought. Now he won't find those white balls until spring. One afternoon during the thaw Arlene will look out the back window and see a field of softballs growing, probably think it was hail. Hail in mud season.

Sheriff Odie Dorfmann, champion pitcher of the Round Corners Royals, paused for a moment, looked up into the sky at the snowflakes peacefully dropping to earth. He wiped a hand across his eyes, then shrugged and stepped back into the batter's box.

12

The Answer to Prayer: What Is the Question?

Personally, George, I believe this is a plot hatched by Odie's titmouse-size brain to coerce me into painting again.

This whole berserk act. Our crack lawman has discovered footprints in the snow around his garage and has deduced that someone jumped up and down on the roof of his workshop, intentionally sabotaging his birdhouses and creative impulses. This is the first time Odie's ever admitted to any creative impulses. He's arresting every suspect that he can think of who holds a grudge against him or simply hates birdhouses.

This pity I feel for Odie is not natural. There's something wrong with it, as if the laws of nature have been turned upside down, as if the sun, the moon, and the stars have been flipped, as if the enemy has somehow developed an interminable disease and has only a month to live. How can you fight with someone like that?

I didn't get along with Odie, long before you showed up, George. I wasn't jealous that you spent all your time with Odie playing softball. Don't flatter yourself, George; the whole world doesn't revolve around you.

Why not?

This is why I never had the desire to paint George. The canvas hasn't been made yet to contain his ego. I ought to tell him I saw Odie cry that day he popped a bucket of fly balls into the snow. That would crush him. George wouldn't believe it. Their friendship was built on a garish, fake jewel foundation of male bonding, both so afraid of showing softness to the other.

I forgot there was softness in Odie until I saw him step into the snowy batter's box, just as I tend to forget there were places that could be hurt in George, too. Maybe that's what went wrong with George and me. Those last years he was so strong, his life so together, while mine was a five-hundred-piece jigsaw puzzle being assembled by a toddler.

What am I painting? This, George, is the map of the road to insanity or inspiration. Another name? Odie.

I know it looks like a cow wearing a holster and gun. It's still evolving. Evolution into a brighter, better species is not a dime-store magic trick. It takes time. And a lot of paint.

When I think back to the days that followed the destruction of Odie's birdhouses, it is like looking at a Jackson Pollock. I see colors whirling and mixing. I see chaos, growing, exploding, flinging trouble a million different directions.

Maybe it was the season, that preholiday depression Wynn reads about in her magazines. Or maybe it was something in the atmosphere, something Thomas couldn't spot with his telescope but was still there entering our hearts and minds like space dust.

Whatever it was I didn't like it—that craziness in the air. Suddenly I wasn't the town wreck anymore. Others were gaining on me in that department.

T-Bone grew a beard. Instead of updating the health records of his herd, he played video games on his computer. He made an effort to look after the cows, simply because he couldn't have Thomas showing him up in his own backyard, but he no longer truly *cared* for them. He couldn't feel the special bond they once had. He hobbled around the house on his crutches, not even trying to walk on his own. When he planted himself in front of the computer, his fingers danced on the computer keys. The tap dance of the barn had been replaced with the ballet of Pac-Man and Donkey Kong.

Wynn stopped doing her pelvic squeezes. Her husband Harvey hadn't opened a baby book in weeks. They seemed to argue about the most insignificant things, such as who put the

ketchup in the refrigerator. Apparently, in the Winchester
household, dipping hot french fries in cold ketchup was a major
offense.

Ella refused to send out Christmas cards until the Postal
Service gave employee discounts for bulk mail. Everyone knew it
was an excuse. She hadn't written poetry, not one line, since the
disappearance of "Howling Mad Home." A Christmas card from
the Snowdens wouldn't be the same without Ella's verses.

And Odie continued on his law and order rampage. He ran in
every drifter that crossed his path. Everyone arrested was sub-
jected to the same treatment: no telephone calls, no food, and
no water until after interrogation. Odie grilled his prisoners
mercilessly under the glare of a single sixty-watt bulb. What, he
demanded, size shoe do you wear, and are you afraid of heights?
The bulb was Wisconsin Dell Addleberry's idea.

The prisoners stood up well under questioning. They thought
the heat from that sixty-watt bulb felt wonderful. They turned
their frozen faces up to the light, as if it were Florida sunshine.
Odie was forced to drag some of them away from the interroga-
tion room. "Didn't bring you here to get a tan," Odie growled. As
for the denied telephone call, that was OK, too. Few of them had
friends who owned homes much less phones. Even fewer had a
lawyer on retainer. But the food and water were another matter.
They had been living on stale saltines and cat food stolen from
camps and were ready for gourmet fixings on the county's bill.
They grew loud and demanding. To get rid of three particularly
exacting suspects, Odie paid for bus tickets to Boston out of his
own pocket.

T-Bone prayed as he never prayed in a pew at Our Lady of
Perpetual Savings. He prayed as he had as a child. The only way
to pray when one has left spiritual matters too late: desperately.
As I leaned against the wall of the barn and listened to T-Bone
and the vet examine the sick cow, I thought of T-Bone's story
about his sixth birthday. When he was six, the parish priest,
Father Julian, gave him a medal of the Virgin Mary blessed by

the Holy Father himself. And when T-Bone wanted something, he would lie in bed at night and rub the medal between his fingers like a rabbit's foot. Once his brother caught him at it and teased him until T-Bone threw the medal out the window just to show how little it meant to him. The next day, when no one was looking, he went out and pawed in the snow, but T-Bone never found the medal.

The veterinarian rose from his stooped position over the cow lying in the stall, wiped his hands, shook his head.

"You almost lost this one, T-Bone."

T-Bone nodded.

"How's your milk production?"

"Low," T-Bone said.

"But she's the only one down?"

"So far."

"I'll give her an injection, and we'll change her feed. I'll look at the rest, while I'm here."

T-Bone nodded.

"You should have called me earlier," the veterinarian said.

Once T-Bone would have noticed a problem long before the cow went down, would have seen the indications, perhaps even known a cow was feeling poorly from the look in its eyes. How close a farmer gets to his animals when he loves his work. But T-Bone no longer knew his cows. He looked at them and saw strangers. There was no rapport; their care had become a chore. T-Bone was ashamed of the estrangement.

A farmer lived with death, but he did not like it. And when he lost, because of his own negligence, a half ton of prime milk machine, a beast that had put food on his table and clothes on his back, a creature that had depended on him for the simplest of kindnesses—a little attention—which he had failed to give, a man didn't stop kicking himself for a long time.

The veterinarian left. "The wife's dragging me to some party, so I better clean up good." She warned him she was not taking the smell of barn to the party. T-Bone and I stayed with the cow. Waiting. In the past, in a situation like this, T-Bone would be going over everything that happened to see what he could have done differently. This time he performed no postmortem on his actions. He knew what he had done.

He stroked the cow, whispering softly to it in French. He apologized for his own stupidity. He should have called the veterinarian earlier. He should have suspected illness. Instead, T-Bone had attributed the drop in milk production to the radio.

T-Bone didn't play the radio anymore.

Long after the cow began to breathe easier and day edged into night, we sat in the silent barn, together, but alone. I lifted T-Bone's hand and placed it against my cheek.

"Do you think the radio is like the medal, Maud? Is it superstition or faith? You know, I broke my mother's favorite bowl after losing the medal, and I never got what I prayed for: that space aliens would come and take my brother away in the middle of the night."

That Sunday T-Bone refused to come to church with us. Once T-Bone was a regular churchgoer. Reverend Samuel Swan called and offered to come over and pray with T-Bone. But T-Bone said no, he'd handle that himself.

So Thomas and I sat alone in the old wooden pews of Our Lady of Perpetual Savings. Thomas made it a practice to attend service in whatever church was nearby when Sunday rolled around. He plans to try all the denominations of the world, he says. Raised with no religious affiliation, not Catholic nor Baptist nor Buddhist, he prefers to call himself a student of the theology of life.

"Sounds like you don't believe in anything," Wynn said one day while cooking chili in my kitchen.

"Officially," Thomas said, "I'm uncommitted."

I handed Wynn the chili powder, admiring the way she shook out a bit in the palm of her hand and nonchalantly flung it into the pot. Amazing, she didn't even use a measuring spoon. "Raj," I said, "told me spirituality has many names and many lives."

"Raj," Wynn said, sprinkling cumin into the chili, "was a fruitcake."

I smiled at the back of Wynn's head, two pews in front of us. She'd styled her hair differently, in some kind of Gibson girl bun. She thought she didn't look motherly enough when it was hanging loose around her shoulders. I turned back to Reverend Swan. He was doing all right today. Everyone knew he fought a constant battle with the devil, time (there was never enough to play his saxophone), and stage fright.

Like me, Reverend Swan was not a fan of numbers. He didn't know how to handle them, not in his bankbook nor in church. For thirty years, he had been preaching, and still he became sick with anticipation before every sermon. Every Sunday he faced his parishioners with the ardent desire to leave the pulpit.

Every day he prayed for courage. He wished he could fling off shyness and pace the sanctuary like the preachers on television. He envied other ministers who burned with the spirit, who so easily stirred up the storm of truth and life. He studied those men on the Christian network, how they rolled up their shirtsleeves and got down to preaching. By their very appearance, they said salvation was work, manual labor, a job they knew how to do. They knew how to talk and walk and act. They knew what to do with their hands, when to reach out to the sky and grasp the moment. They moved and their steps echoed in the hearts of men. And their voices: Where did they learn to talk like that? Where did they learn to roll those r's in "redemption" and "repent"?

Reverend Swan cleared his throat and looked out onto the congregation. He saw many familiar faces. The Snowdens, Wynn and Harvey, Freda Lee and her children, Odie and Arlene, the Smiths, the Joneses, the Browns, Wisconsin Dell Addleberry, me.

"You are among friends," his wife always reminded him. She sat, as usual, in the front pew. She caught his attention and smiled. She tried to make things easier for him. He knew, with her smile, she was trying to flood him with confidence, as in those pictures of the saints where the light pours from heaven onto their heads.

I suspected that at times like this Reverend Swan regretted his conversion. His life would have been so much easier if he had stayed a Catholic and let the pope tell him what to do. "Have you ever noticed," he once asked his wife, "how positive priests are about everything?" Of course, he couldn't have married Mrs. Swan if he had remained Catholic and become a priest. And he did so love Mrs. Swan. When Reverend Swan gazed upon his wife's face, he thought maybe this weekly hell was worth it.

Like Reverend Swan, the Church of Our Lady of Perpetual Savings once had been Catholic. Years ago it was traded to the Episcopalians for a piece of land up the mountain. The Catholics at the time had outgrown the church and wanted to build a bigger one; they had a fat building fund. The Episcopalians, on the other hand, had the Reverend Samuel Swan.

Reverend Swan was not good at asking people for money. His wife said he was a marvelous minister, but he left much to be desired as a fund-raiser. So the Episcopalians had only one asset: a plot of land left to the congregation in the will of a founding member. To a following that met in the wintry basement of the library on cold, metal folding chairs, the Catholic proposal was quite appealing.

The trade was made.

The Church of Our Lady of Perpetual Savings was not its real name. It started as just the Church of Our Lady more than one hundred years ago. Then one year, the Round Corners First Savings and Loan next door burned down, taking with it two bank officers who gave their lives to save the safety deposit boxes. They slammed themselves in the big fireproof vault. They thought they would be safe. The coroner said it must have heated up hotter than hell in the huge steel chamber.

The browned, flame-licked vault was moved temporarily to the church until a new structure could be built. The Catholics, who still owned the church at the time and who were never ones to turn their backs on money, saw no problem in opening the vestibule for banking hours. For the eight months it took to construct a new building on the site of the old bank, Round

Corners residents deposited their paychecks and prayers at what came to be called Our Lady of Perpetual Savings.

Our Lady of Perpetual Savings was the only church in town now. The Catholics took a beating in the sixties, their population dropping significantly with the advent of free love and the Vietnam War. Large numbers of younger parishioners migrated legally to California and illegally to Canada. The church on the mountain became too big for its congregation; it was renovated, keeping the chapel but turning the rest into a restaurant and cross-country ski center.

Perhaps, because Our Lady was the only church in the area, Reverend Swan thought he should provide an ecumenical message. In the congregation were Catholics, Presbyterians, Unitarians, even a Baptist. In winter, the church served the ski crowd, and only God knew what they were. So although Reverend Swan considered himself Episcopalian, he tended to criss-cross church lines, a theological skier.

Reverend Swan tried to relax the hands clutching the sides of the pulpit, where he knew men of sureness had stood for centuries. Once, he told me, he could almost feel their footprints in that worn spot behind the pulpit. They were men who made their mark. Real men of God seldom have doubts, Reverend Swan knew. Reverend Swan took a breath, looked out on the people, and wished he'd landed that seat in the Bibleland Band.

"Today I'd like to talk about forgiveness . . ."

Two days after Reverend Swan's stirring sermon on forgiveness, Harvey Winchester knocked on my door and asked to see Wynn.

Wynn and I were arguing over who would decorate the tops of the cupcakes she had just baked. She wanted pink frosting squirted in the shape of a snowflake atop each cupcake.

"You're the artist here, Maud," she said with exasperation.

"I don't do cupcakes."

"You are an artistic snob."

"All right, give me the damn cupcakes," I shouted, answering the door.

"No, with your attitude, you'd probably ruin them, make snowflakes that look like cows or something."

"Low blow, Wynn."

Wynn was surprised to see Harvey. "Why aren't you at work?" She completed a snowflake. "You're always at work, it seems lately."

"Wynn . . ." Harvey said, nervously playing with his baseball cap.

"What?"

"Wynn," Harvey cleared his throat. "I have something to tell you."

"It must be something important to take off work." Wynn glanced at him sharply. "You're not sick?"

"No, no," Harvey said quickly. "I have a confession to make, Wynn." Harvey pulled at his collar. "Is it warm in here?"

"It's just fine in here, Harvey Mandelson Winchester. What is the matter with you?" Wynn asked.

Harvey took a running start and made the leap. "Ileftyour prizewinningknittingneedlesonthewoodstoveandmeltedthem."

Wynn froze, her hand holding the squirt tube of frosting above the cupcake. She didn't look at Harvey. Slowly, carefully, she whispered, "What did you say?"

Harvey rushed to her side, but held back from touching her. "I melted your prize-winning knitting needles on the woodstove."

"The ones half of Round Corners is looking for?" Wynn's voice rose with each word. "The subjects of a criminal investigation by Sheriff Odie Dorfmann? The ones I have been dying to find for months?"

Harvey swallowed. "Those are the ones."

Silence.

"You see they were lying on the stove and I started building a fire and I was reading one of those baby books and I just didn't pay attention to what I was doing, Wynn. Honest to God," he glanced to me for help. I shrugged. "I didn't mean to do it. It was an accident. Please believe me; it was an accident."

"What took you so long to tell me?"

"I was scared."

Wynn almost looked at him then, but she kept her head down. "I don't think I want to talk to you right now, Harvey."

"Wynn."

"And you'll have to go to the Round Corners Restaurant tonight for dinner. There won't be any at our house."

"Wynn."

"Not now, Harvey."

Harvey turned to me, but I shook my head. I touched his arm and guided him toward the door. "Talk to her, Maud," he begged as he climbed into his truck.

I took the tube of frosting from Wynn and finished the snowflakes. She sniffled. "I'm going to eat every one of these cupcakes, Maud. I don't care if this baby weighs as much as a humpback whale when it arrives; I'm going to have all the chocolate I want tonight. And don't try to stop me."

"Wouldn't think of it."

I rolled Wynn out to her car around midnight. Harvey spent the intervening hours too worried to eat more than two bites of his Salisbury steak plate at the Round Corners Restaurant; he couldn't watch television, so he watched the window. When Wynn arrived home, she still wasn't talking to him. They crawled into bed in silence.

During the night, Wynn was sick from two dozen chocolate cupcakes with pink snowflakes banging around inside her. Harvey held her hair back as she leaned over the commode and emptied her stomach. He gently wiped her face with a cool cloth, stroking away the tears on her cheeks. He helped her back to bed. And after a moment, he spooned up behind her, holding her softly against him. She let him. And Harvey sighed.

13

Even Lovers Get the Blues

Snowflakes do not fall silently. They make sounds, depending on where you are. Standing in the middle of the woods, they sound like sparkling wind, groaning pines, and snoring filtering up from the deeply buried burrows of little creatures. In the Round Corners Restaurant, they sound like the bell of the cash register.

It had snowed every day since Thanksgiving, and ski conditions were irresistible. The ski patrol practically had to throw the skiers off the slopes at the end of the day. They had to shovel them off the ice rink with the Zamboni machine. Skiers and skaters stomped into the café tired and ravenous, carrying snowflakes on their shoulders. Their sunburned, wind-chapped cheeks glowed. Their laughter was weary but happy.

With every jangle of the bell over the door, I looked up. T-Bone promised he would be in tonight. I heard the door again and spun around. But it was Odie, standing by the register where long ago the Maud Calhoun greeting cards had run out. He squeezed onto a stool next to Amos and motioned for a coffee.

I served two filet mignons to a booth by the window. "Anything else?" I asked, slamming the plates down in front of two skiers. They looked at each other. "No," they said quickly, "everything's fine, looks delicious."

I slid a cup of coffee in front of Odie and swung into the kitchen, running into cross fire between Freda Lee and the kid cook. They were going round and round over a plate of cold french fries.

"If you picked up your orders once in a while, this wouldn't happen," said the kid.

"I'm in here two seconds after you hit that damn bell you play like a set of drums."

"I've got a bottle of molasses back here that runs faster than you, Freda Lee."

"Listen, kid, you're the one who's too lazy to fry up a fresh batch of fries. These are cold and leftover. Now, give me some fresh ones before I cut you up into little pieces and throw you in the fryer."

"Bitch."

Freda lifted her head, grabbed a pot of scalding coffee, and headed for the swinging door.

"What's the matter, Freda Lee," the kid sniped, "not getting enough from that bum you live with?"

Freda made an abrupt turn and went for the cook with the coffee. He jumped back as I leapt forward, catching Freda's arm and taking the coffeepot from her. Gently, I returned it to the warmer.

"Have those fries ready when I get back," I told the cook, who quickly forgot his fear and began to pout. "Come on," I snatched Freda's arm and pulled her into the back room.

We shoved bags of onions and flour aside and perched on two five-gallon cans of lard. Freda lit a cigarette. I waited. "Lousy kid," Freda said, "lousy, smart-assed kid. I hate people who think they know so much about life, and they don't know shit. They're just as dumb as the day they were born. Fucking kid. What does he know of loving somebody?"

"Nobody could love more than you and Lewis Lee."

"You're damn right. Nobody. What does he know about keeping a family together?"

The bell in the kitchen called. *Ding ding ding.*

"He doesn't know shit." Freda studied the tip of her cigarette. "He doesn't have an inkling of what it's like to lose something important to you, something that keeps you going, that makes your day worth waking up to, that keeps you from going off half crazy and getting a job."

"Lewis Lee's got a job?" *Ding ding ding.*

"Stuff it!" Freda yelled. She exhaled. "Driving trucks, logging trucks, to New Hampshire and back. He's gone all the time it seems. I'm used to having him around." She blew out a long, slow stream of smoke. "Maud, I got spoiled. My Lord, the fun we'd have in the afternoons watching the soap operas."

"But why? Why did he get a job?"

Freda said Lewis Lee had had a change of heart about life. He lost his knife and couldn't whittle any little figures for her and the kids' Christmas presents, so he decided to earn the money for gifts.

"I wanted to buy him another whittling knife, but Lewis said it wouldn't be the same. His father gave him that knife when he was a boy. It was his grandfather's before that." Freda puffed furiously on the cigarette and wearily exhaled. Her eyes watered as if the smoke had blown back into her face instead of drifting my way.

"I told him the kids and me don't need gifts," she whispered so softly I had to lean closer to hear. "But he won't listen. I miss the old Lewis Lee, the one who didn't crawl in bed too tired to even talk, the one who laughed under the covers and said silly things. I loved that man. This one just isn't the same."

Ding ding ding.

I patted Freda's shoulder. "You're right, some people don't know shit about life."

Odie unzipped his down parka, institutional green as it was part of the Round Corners Police Department's official uniform; the nylon rustled as he reached for five sugar packets, tapped them against his finger, and ripped off the tops. All five went into his coffee.

"Pass on the cream, Maud. Arlene's been nagging about my weight again." Odie sipped his coffee. "Can you believe it about Harvey Winchester? Pretty damn sad when a man's afraid to talk to his wife. Then again when Wynn's the wife, it may be understandable. She can be a wild woman, and pregnancy has not turned her into Miss Congeniality. Once I was in the shop for a haircut, and she kept me waiting while she ripped out some stitches on that kid's afghan."

"Mothers," Amos said.

"Mothers," agreed Bartholomew.

"I think this whole town's gone nuts," Odie said. "I hope you ain't been painting all this crazy stuff that's been going on, Maud."

I smiled. "I've been painting it; Ella's been writing it. When we're finished with Round Corners, it's going to make Peyton Place look like kindergarten." Odie sputtered, spitting his coffee across the counter.

Frank and Ella came in and took a booth behind Odie, Amos, and Bartholomew. Frank kept his back to the wall. It was hamburger steak night, Frank's favorite.

"Two of the usual?" I asked, pouring their coffees.

"Yes," Frank said.

"No," Ella said.

Frank glared at her; she stared him down.

"I want something different. We don't have to have hamburger steak all the time. The world isn't going to end if I have a grilled cheese."

"It's a good night for grilled cheese," I said. Frank and Ella remained silent. "And for hamburger steak."

It was obvious that Frank and Ella weren't talking to each other. Which meant they doubly didn't want to talk to Odie. So I could have doused Odie with decaf when he leaned over and said, "Well, your employer has gotten himself in a mess now, Ella."

Ella ruffled up like an offended bird. She had given up trying to explain to Odie that the Postal Service was a private business and not a branch of the United States government. Odie subscribed to selective memory and identification. When the government did something he agreed with, it was "his country." When it did something he considered absurd, it was "Ella's boss."

"Oh, really?"

"Can't turn on the news without hearing about that cruise

ship being held hostage out in the middle of the Atlantic Ocean."

Sea-jacked by terrorists, the Star in Heaven, the special cruise filled with the world's greatest astronomers, had hogged the headlines for days. Thomas was supposed to have been on that cruise, but changed his mind. He wasn't ready to leave Round Corners yet, he said. So he missed the boat.

"Oh, that," Ella sighed. "Terrible, isn't it?"

"Thomas is fit to be tied," I said. "He's glued to CNN."

"You can't blame him. All those innocent stargazers." Ella tutted.

Odie shook his head. "The government has to make a move. Send in the frogmen or something."

"They don't want to endanger the passengers," Ella argued.

"I'd send in sharpshooters myself. They have guys who can plug a hole right through those terrorists' tonsils. They'd never know what hit them."

"How would they get close enough to the boat?"

"I'd send them in on dolphins. They're the smartest creatures in the world."

"Too smart to get mixed up in that harebrained scheme."

"So what's your idea? Talk them into trading a luxury cruise liner for a cozy little jail cell? Read them a poem? Appeal to their literary sensibility? Ella, all I got to say is: It's a good thing the world isn't run by pacifist poets like you. I don't blame Frank for barricading that door one bit. Should have done it years ago."

Ella gasped. The whole town knew about Ella and Frank's terrible fight. The root of the argument was Frank's misguided remarks about Ella's memory. Actually, it was not the remarks themselves, but the fact that Frank had yet to apologize for making them. Ella could excuse words uttered in the heat of the moment, but she could not forgive ill manners.

Each day his words ate at her until one morning she reached the point where she didn't care what kind of eyes—hotcakes, Quaker Oats, or lumpy Cream of Wheat—Frank looked at her with, he wasn't getting anything.

"Aren't we having breakfast this morning?" Frank said.

"I am," said Ella, pulling a hot plate of bacon and eggs out of the oven. She took the plate to the table, sat down, and arranged a napkin in her lap.

Frank could see the steam wafting off the fluffy scrambled eggs. He smelled the dash of vanilla Ella always used. His wife made the best scrambled eggs.

He peeked in the oven. "Where's mine?"

Ella ignored him.

Frank looked at the scrambled eggs again—they were practically smoking—and headed for the shower. As he passed behind Ella, he said in a casual voice, "I think I'll have breakfast at the store. I feel like some of those gooey, flaky bear claws."

Ella's fork clanged against the plate. He knew she loved bear claws better than life itself, almost. Certainly better than Frank Snowden at that moment.

She rushed to the bathroom door and banged on it. No answer. Just the sounds of waterfall, pouring out of their new Shower Massage attachment, and Frank singing. Each morning he used every last drop of water in the tank rehearsing barbershop quartet songs. Ella hammered again with her fist.

"Frank, I'm tired of performing my ablutions at night because you use all the hot water in the morning, and I'm tired of you performing those awful songs at the crack of dawn."

The shower shut off. Silence. Ella placed her ear against the door. No singing, no buzz of electric shaver, no rattle of the loose towel rack. Suddenly, the door was flung open, and Ella almost fell into the bathroom. Frank strolled out of the bathroom in a waft of steam and hothouse nonchalance.

"Ella," he said, "I'm going to eat the whole box of bear claws myself."

Before it was over, Ella ended up at my house, blubbering while she posed, retelling the whole story again and again as if her broken heart was a broken record. Meanwhile, Frank drove to Snowden's General Store and set to building a barricade of cans and boxes—beans, spaghetti, toilet paper.

Customers came in and Frank said, "What do you need?"

without so much as a hello. Peanuts, Pringles, they said, and stamps. "I can help you out with the peanuts and Pringles," Frank said. "But you're on your own for the stamps." Frank swung his head to point next door. If they wanted stamps, they had to trudge all the way back outside, climb over the snowbank, and enter the post office through the main door. The shortcut, between one side of the big old building and the other, between grocery and post office, between Frank and Ella, was gone.

I closed up the Round Corners Restaurant without a sign of T-Bone. Thomas was waiting for me in the parking lot. When he saw me, he jumped out of his van, walked over to mine, and opened the door. I regarded him a moment, then climbed in. Thomas followed me home.

We built up the fire in the woodstove, turned off the lights, and for the first time in a week, I tore into a six-pack. I tossed Thomas a beer, and we curled up on opposite ends of the sofa. We drank in the dark, the curtains open, the snowflakes dancing in the spotlight of the outside lamp. I kicked off my shoes and rubbed one foot. "Here, let me," Thomas said, swinging my feet up on his lap. He massaged the arches and ankles and toes. I sighed and closed my eyes.

"You know, I wish I had seen it."

"What?"

"The house."

I didn't open my eyes. "It was something else all right." Thomas's fingers felt so good. "When I was a child, it seemed such a natural place. No matter where I was, if I got the urge, I just pulled a crayon from my pocket (I always had one) and made a picture. It was much like little boys taking a leak in the garden."

Thomas pushed the hair out of his eyes. "Why do I miss everything? Vietnam, the demonstrations, sit-ins, streaking, this house. My mom and dad tell such great stories of the way things were."

"After I married George, I always felt like I was fiddling with it, like a woman who can't help straightening her husband's tie. Of

course, George's ties were never crooked. And it was impossible
to find any lint to pick from his lapel."

"I wish I had seen it."

I leaned forward and patted his cheek. He grabbed my hand
and held it in place. His eyes, in that moment, were like
George's, so expectant, so clear, so simple. He pulled me close.

His lips were soft and gentle, almost hesitant. I felt the experi-
enced one. There was a part of me standing back, uninvolved,
observing. I was ashamed that I had time to think other thoughts,
that the kiss did not command all my brain cells, that I had
energy left over to plot fantasies. I wanted to be mindless. I
wanted to be flame. I wanted to wiggle like a tadpole.

I put my mind to the kiss, frightening Thomas. He paused,
then continued more confidently. I must have done all right. In
the end, I don't think Thomas had a clue what was on my mind:
how nice the words "moon drop" are, how many colors of red
there are, how long the smell of paint lingers in a room.

"You coming to bed?" Thomas asked.

I smiled. "In a bit."

"Oh." He stood uncertainly, then headed for the door.

"Thomas?"

"Yes?"

"I wish you had seen the house, too."

Long after Thomas turned in, I sat by the fire, staring out the
window at the snowflakes caught in the dark by the magic of the
porch light. In a snowstorm, there is great aloneness. There is
coldness even though your back is up against the woodstove.
Suddenly, I wanted to be near T-Bone. I pulled on my boots and
gloves, zipped up my parka, and drove to his farm.

No one answered my knock. I plowed through the snow
around the house. The light in the office shone warmly in the
windows. And there was T-Bone, snoring on the sofa. Cat rode
his sleeping chest. I wanted to pound on the window and
scream, where the hell were you? Instead, I stood there, my toes
growing cold then numb. I stayed until my fingers tingled and
hurt. I stayed—finally understanding the loneliness I had brought

him all these years—to watch over him and to listen to the sizzling silence of the snowflakes.

14

Inevitability Is Owning a China Shop on the New Madrid Fault

Contrary to popular belief, we do not have Clydesdales hanging out on every corner in Vermont. We don't slice through the snow in curlicue sleighs drawn by big draft horses with jingling harnesses. We get to the grocery, the laundromat, the bowling alley like most people do—with front-wheel drive. But you can't tell the tourists anything.

To them, this is Clydesdale Country. This is, according to Hollywood, the home of holiday nostalgia; the good old days are still good here, still scented with pine wreaths and spiced cider. The cold evenings smell of smoke from the woodstoves. Sleds lean against the back door. Meals are long and the drink is potent. Guests are not eager to leave the table, bundle up, pump the cold accelerator, and arrive home just as the heater warms up. So they stay and they laugh and the children play nicely under the Christmas tree.

That, says George and Hollywood, is the stuff of beer commercials. George was not alone in his belief in marketing the New England mystique. Round Corners lost its first bid for fame five years ago when a beer company that shall remain nameless chose a town to the east as the site for its seasonal filmmaking. George insisted then that the Round Corners business community simply hadn't put together a competitive economic development package. He whined about how the other town had offered free accommodations for the film crew at the local ski lodge, an attractive tax-incentive package, and a year's supply of Vermont maple syrup for the producer.

And so, naturally, George was miffed when Round Corners

caught the eye of Hollywood (or is it Milwaukee?). A year after
George the economic developer died, Round Corners was
selected as the site for "Clydesdale II: The Sequel."

Rotten luck, George, to die like that before you even had a
crack at stardom. All right, I'll tell you about it. I won't leave
out a thing. I'll concentrate. I know details are important,
George. Jesus, you're talking to an artist.

Hollywood turned Round Corners upside down and inside
out. Ella refused to be one of the carolers, because Frank was
leading the group. Wynn, who had been wearing Harvey's parka
because it was the only coat she could find that buttoned over her
growing stomach, said she wouldn't be filmed in army green;
finally the script woman (a size eighteen) lent Wynn a pink ski
jacket. And Thomas said forget about the Peace Corps; he was
considering a career as a beer commercial director.

The film crew arrived in town a week ago and hired every-
one in town to play the crowd scenes. Equity pay scale,
George. Yes, for everyone, except Odie. He landed a speak-
ing role as the sleigh driver. What does he say? "Whoa!"

I'm sure you would have been a better sleigh driver,
George.

We've been rehearsing all week. No, not because Odie
can't remember his line. It's difficult working with animals. It
just takes longer dealing with pet stars. How many? Well,
there's the horses and the dog. I didn't mention the dog? I
know that's a detail. The dog has a crucial role. He runs
along beside the sleigh, barking happily, welcoming his
family home after a long day cruising around in the snow
spreading holiday cheer.

The problem? Well, it seems the dog doesn't like Odie. He
keeps lifting his leg when Odie is around. Odie has warned
the dog boy, that's the kid in charge of seeing that the dog
has everything it needs, that he'll run him in on a misde-
meanor (Mishandling of Toxic Wastes, or MTW in Wisconsin
Dell's lingo) if he doesn't keep his pooper-scooper handy.

Yes, George, the dog would have loved you. I recall you

*were a friend to the entire animal world. Saint Francis of
Round Corners's wild kingdom.*

That afternoon we filmed.

The scene featured a group of carolers, led by Frank
Snowden and accompanied by Reverend Swan on the saxo-
phone. Take after take, we sang the same song, "Jingle Bells."
The afternoon wore on and the temperature dropped and the
cold carolers began to shuffle their L.L. Bean boots. The director
begged us to be still; the soundman complained that his high-
tech equipment picked up every creak and groan.

Finally, we sang a perfect "Jingle Bells" and were allowed to
go home and warm our toes by the fire. Reverend Swan care-
fully packed away his saxophone and leaned it against a tree by
the curb. He mingled among the professional musicians, hired
and bused in from Burlington by the director. He was totally
enamored of those showbiz types.

"Tomorrow we'll shoot the scene in front of the Crawford's
place," the director told Odie.

Odie nodded. "I'll be there bright and early for my makeup
call."

"Good," the director said, "because someone's got to take
down all those goddamn birdhouses. There must be ten of them
in the Crawford's yard."

"The birdhouses?"

"They're ruining the shot. Too tacky. Tacky as plastic fla-
mingos."

"Tacky!" roared Odie. "One of those houses is an exact
replica of the Babe's home. Babe Ruth, y'know, the world's
greatest baseball player of all time."

The director wasn't listening. "Thank God, the Crawfords
didn't put up some of those cardboard figures of fat farmwives
bending over the garden picking tomatoes and showing their
pantaloons."

"Cardboard farmwives?"

"The birdhouses go. See to it, will you, Sheriff?"

Odie stared at the director, who already had moved on to brief the camera crew about tomorrow's schedule. Odie's face reddened, his eyes bulged; it was like looking at Wile E. Coyote after he swallowed a stick of TNT. Not aware of the impending explosion, Ella approached Odie about buying a Christmas wreath for the county jail. Ella's book club, a group of elderly women who got together once a month to discuss books and exchange recipes, were making and selling wreaths as a fund-raiser for the library. Odie ignored Ella, sidestepped around her, and stalked to his police car. The engine roared, and the car spun 180 degrees, backed into a tree, and peeled out in a shower of snow. "That man is getting nearly impossible to talk to," huffed Ella.

I spun on my heel, hearing running footsteps behind me, crunching the snow. "Oh, no," Reverend Swan cried. Reverend Swan knelt by the tree Odie had just creamed. Both hands clawed frantically at the trunk. Finally, they peeled away a layer of leather and metal, some compacted cartoon of Reverend Swan's saxophone.

"Oh, no," I said.

I walked a silent Reverend Swan home, handed him over to Mrs. Swan, explained about the saxophone lying in his arms like a broken child. Reverend Swan didn't answer his wife when she called his name. His eyes were blank and unblinking. I shivered, probably suffering from too many takes of "Jingle Bells," I said. Gently, Mrs. Swan wrapped her arm around her husband and led him into the house. Before she closed the door, I heard her say, "This can be fixed. The Lord doesn't give us anything that can't be fixed."

Unlike Mrs. Swan, I don't believe life comes with a warranty. As the eloquent say, "Shit happens." Things get broken. Humpty Dumpty, promises, cups in a china shop on the New Madrid fault. You can fix them, but they're never the same. They have hairline cracks. Disaster waiting to happen.

After George died, T-Bone insisted I install a telephone in the studio. "What if you fell in a bucket of paint and drowned," he said. "You could lie in a puddle of purple mountain majesty, semigloss, for days, and no one would know."

If I had a phone, he said, he could check on me.

So I bought the damn phone.

And now he doesn't use it.

I skidded the van to a stop in T-Bone's yard and rammed the gear stick into park. I hadn't heard from T-Bone in two days, since he got off the crutches. Thomas said not to take it personally. "He's getting accustomed to the cane," Thomas said. I was spoiling for a fight, cripple or not.

The day T-Bone finished with the crutches, he told Thomas he could manage the milking by himself now. Fine, Thomas said. But the next morning, out of habit, Thomas drove over to T-Bone's. As soon as he pulled into the yard, he heard the cows bawling. It was close to seven, and they hadn't been milked yet. He found T-Bone asleep in bed.

I jumped out of the van, slammed the door, headed for the barn, then skidded to a stop. Music drifted from the barn. Music, I smiled. I pictured T-Bone waltzing between the stalls, the straw acting as rosin. His feet were machines, tireless. Tapping and tapping and tapping.

I imagined his lithe figure swirling and dodging among the cows, like Farmer Fred Astaire, and forgot about being mad at him. One year the college where Harvey Winchester grooms the lawns and shovels the sidewalks sponsored a Fred Astaire film festival. Twice a week for a whole month, T-Bone and I motored twenty miles to the college to see movies such as *Silk Stockings, Daddy Long Legs,* and *Funny Face.*

T-Bone loved to watch Astaire dance with brooms and firecrackers and magical shoes. I preferred Astaire solo, when his only prop was his body, a loaded gun ready to shatter the continuum of space and light. Run away and come back. It was a game. One moment he appeared fighting for control, the next gliding on glass. Run away and come back. It was an art. His body loved to move, as did T-Bone's.

I heard the music and gave a skip. The old T-Bone was back.
It feels good, surprisingly good. It feels like coming home. At last,
I thought, we can go back to the way we were.

Inside the milking parlor, the temperature is kept at a constant
winter temperature of forty-five degrees Fahrenheit. T-Bone said
cows cannot be expected to give their best milk when you have
to knock the icicles off their udders. I love T-Bone's barn. The
warmth wraps around you like wet wool.

I paused in the doorway of his barn, grinning. I had to force
myself to be quiet, I was so excited. Maybe I could catch him
dancing, sneak a few moments of just looking at him, of observ-
ing the ebb and flow of his dancing body.

I silently stepped into the big barn.

Slowly, the smile slid from my face, like a single melted tear.

T-Bone stumbled. He shuffled, his joints stiff, his balance
precarious, his body leaden. The flirting game between man and
gift was gone, taken by an ax on a chilly afternoon. His beautiful
body would not cooperate. It refused to shape the light. Space
slipped through its grasp, like sand through spread fingers.
Gravity in the barn seemed to have doubled, tripled.

I could taste frustration in the barn, growing, rising with the
music and the missteps, filling to the rafters, reaching into the
cobwebbed corners. "T-Bone," I cried, but no words passed my
lips. I watched helplessly for what seemed like hours. Finally,
T-Bone gave up. He stood in the middle of the cows, shoulders
slumped, hands clenched in fists. He sighed and flung back his
head, as if seeking divine intervention. Instead, he got me.

"Can I buy you a beer?" I asked, stepping out of the shadows.
I approached carefully. He watched me, not bothering to dash a
tear from his cheek. I stopped a breath away from him. "With
chips."

"No Doritos."

"No Doritos," I said, tiptoeing to wipe the moisture from his
cheek.

Suddenly he grabbed me and wrapped me in a mighty bear
hug. He burrowed his head in my shoulder and whispered over

and over, "What am I to do? What am I to do?" His arms were so strong and so desperate. I wanted to give him everything then, every piece of light in the world. Perhaps he had always needed me like this, and I didn't realize it. Perhaps I had always needed him.

T-Bone's bedroom. The colors are so solid here, so deep. Forest greens and burgundies hold secrets and safety. Woodland colors. It seems natural to be here, T-Bone gripping my hand in his sleep. I am a sucker for vulnerable men. My father who could never figure out one end of a Picasso from the other. George who could only be hurt by nonperformance, by the stillness of a paintbrush, by people who gave up. Thomas who feels so out of place here and so at home talking to the night stars.

Love really is like a country-and-western song. In every toughness there is weakness. In every icicle there is the essence of glacier. We live for momentous sparks. For nanoseconds of invulnerability. But we are loved for the little things, the way we wear green suede cowboy boots, the way we see potential in an old gutted van in a field of trillium, the way we help a neighbor stack his woodpile.

The air is cold. I am good at putting off that mad race against the cold to the woodstove, that fumbling with iron door and heavy wood while bouncing from one cold foot to another. T-Bone sighed in his sleep and mumbled, "I have always loved you, y'know." I threw my leg over T-Bone's and snuggled closer. In the shadow of T-Bone's warmth, I tried to forget the sound of Odie taking an ax to the birdhouses at the Crawford place. The Crawford place is five miles away. Funny how I can still hear the ax; the jingling harnesses of bored, restless horses; how I can hear a man's heart break.

In every toughness there is weakness, and that weakness, Hollywood, is the stuff of art.

15

Dashing through the Snow in a Horse-Drawn Ice Cube Tray

Christmas draws a full house at the Church of Our Lady of Perpetual Savings. Only Easter beats it for numbers. People feel the need to get their spiritual houses in order at the end of the year, Reverend Swan says.

Sandwiched between T-Bone and Thomas, I feel at peace, more content than I have felt in a long time. Both T-Bone and Thomas were there under duress. Thomas wanted to stay home and watch a PBS show on black holes and comets, and T-Bone just wanted to stay home period. I leaned closer to T-Bone; our thighs touched. I enjoyed T-Bone's warmth, running like a stripe down the side of my body.

Thomas flipped through the hymnal. On the way to church, all three of us scrunched in the front seat of Thomas's yellow van, Thomas described some of the churches from his travels. "Some wouldn't be considered churches in Round Corners. One was just an adobe box with a flat roof. Inside were candles and incense burners and pictures of Buddha and Christ. I suspect divinity diplomas were sold out of the room in the back."

"Our Lady of Perpetual Savings does not have a degree program," I said.

"Probably not," Thomas smiled. "Its foundation is rock and prayer, its architecture purely Puritan. Notice how it's built, in such a way as to direct everything—eyes, thought, soul—upward. The windows are high; the suffering of the saints depicted in stained glass let in nothing of brightness—neither sunlight nor inspiration. Steps lead up to the sanctuary. White steeple leads up to heaven. Nothing encourages a person to look to the side, not in actuality nor in philosophy."

"Aw shit," T-Bone said, "this is going to be one of those philosophical days, I can just feel it."

Thomas viewed Our Lady much as American tourists considered European cathedrals—more attraction than place of worship. "Holy places," he said, "are the forests and jungles and deserts."

Maybe he was right. Sometimes it is difficult to believe that God would prefer a place like this—with its hard seats and stark white walls, its threadbare rug and loud bells—to the meadows and the ever changing sky, the soft grasses and the musical breezes. God wasn't dumb.

With a crowd like the one at Our Lady on Christmas morning, any other minister would have been happy. Not Reverend Swan. He peered out at all those faces in horror. Later, he confessed he didn't recognize a single one, not even his precious wife, Mrs. Swan. He squinted and ducked his head as if looking into a bright light. He knew Mrs. Swan was out there somewhere; they drove to church together. He'd forgotten to warm up the car. The heater couldn't do much in the short distance from their house to the church. Sitting in the little metal container with bucket seats and vinyl upholstery (the most economical, stripped down model the Swans could find) was like riding in an ice cube tray.

Reverend Swan thought of tiny people crowded into ice cube trays coasting up and down the Green Mountains. He mumbled something about Ethan Allen and his boys freeing this country in horse-drawn ice cube trays. T-Bone and I exchanged uneasy glances. Members of the congregation began to whisper; they shifted uncomfortably in their seats.

Suddenly, Reverend Swan snapped to attention. His focus sharpened, and he saw, for the first time, the restless crowd. They waited, for him.

"I . . ." Reverend Swan said, seemingly at a loss. His hand touched a paper, reminding him of his notes, which he had forgotten earlier in the cold car. He glanced at the index cards that he had dashed out in his vestments to retrieve from the ice cube tray, the notes stacked neatly on the pulpit, and discovered: He couldn't read them. His heart lurched. Struck blind in the middle of a sermon. Surely, there was a sign in that. Who would drive the ice cube tray home? What should he do? Say something. He started talking, rambling, saying whatever came to mind. He could have been discussing grocery lists for all he knew. He squinted at the blurry notes, but they still were no help. Loss. He could tell the congregation about loss. Loss of vision.

"When I was a child, I was always losing things," Reverend Swan said. "Once, in fourth grade at Sacred Heart School, I lost my gloves. At recess, I shuffled to the office in my big snow boots and asked Sister Magdalen if I could look for my gloves in the lost-and-found box. As I pawed through the moldy pile of mittens, hats, scarves, and jackets, Sister Magdalen lectured. She said I should have clipped them to my coat. I should ask the Lord, Sister Magdalen said, to help me to be more conscientious.

"I did not find the gloves and returned to the schoolyard with the distinct impression that loss was a sin and frozen fingers was the penance. I believe I have grown more conscientious with age, but still I keep losing things."

Reverend Swan scratched his head. "Go figure," he mumbled, "go figure."

As the parishioners poured out of Our Lady of Perpetual Savings, the snow dropped like stones from the sky. A silent snow, a holy snow, a purifying snow. It hushed the landscape, slowed the busyness, returned the day to nature and God. In no time, snow covered the shoulders and hair of Reverend Swan, who stood on the steps of the church greeting his flock.

No one seemed in a hurry to head home. We stood in groups on the church steps, chatting, feeling the beautiful softness of the snowflakes on our eyelashes and in our dimples. It felt right to be together at that moment. There was a closeness between humans, between man and nature, between man and God. This, I thought, was what the television producer was trying to capture in his beer commercial—and never would. I was glad. I didn't want Hollywood to take back this piece of Round Corners. It was such a perfect piece, I wondered how even I dared to try to capture it on one of my canvases.

For Christmas dinner, Thomas cooked some vegetarian holiday dish. T-Bone sneaked in three bags of potato chips under his parka. After dinner we watched *It's a Wonderful Life* on television, making sure to flip past those other holiday movies with Fred Astaire in them.

While T-Bone and I cuddled and dodged the holiday musicals, Wynn and Harvey carved the bird with Harvey's mother who undoubtedly made some crack about Wynn's enormous appetite or her hair color. Freda and Lewis Lee watched the children pulverize the pretty wrapping paper under the Christmas tree, and when all the toys were assembled and the kids were squabbling about whose action toy was the best, Freda Lee slipped away to the bathroom where she perched on the commode with a bottle of expensive perfume in her hands, and wondered why she wished it was some silly animal carving made from a clothespin.

Wisconsin Dell manned the dispatcher station as she does all the other 364 days of the year; the day was quiet except for the occasional SSB (Skiers in Snowbank). Between calls for tow trucks, Wisconsin Dell carefully touched the box of chocolates and monogrammed handkerchiefs placed by the microphone where she could see them all day. Every Christmas Odie gives his dispatcher chocolates and monogrammed handkerchiefs, thinking each year this is a new and innovative gift. His dispatcher never corrects him.

Odie pulled two cars full of skiers out of the ditch on his way home from church; while his wife stuffed the turkey, Odie stuffed hundreds of little suet bags and hung them on the trees in his yard as a gift for the birds. The suet bags covered the trees like Christmas bulbs.

Frank and Ella Snowden ate a crispy ham in polite silence; Frank didn't remind Ella that any ham, much less a burned one, isn't his favorite, and Ella didn't say anything about the puddles of melted snow she stepped in with her stocking feet when Frank forgot to take off his boots after church. They exchanged gifts: a red tie for a man who hasn't worn a tie in ten years and a pair of leather racing gloves for a woman who prefers woolen mittens.

On that quiet day, behind every door in Round Corners, there was unquiet. It was that kind of Christmas.

At Christmas, Reverend Swan's flock included more than his regulars. There was a large showing of tourists, people who spent the week of Christmas skiing, people who bought little Christmas trees for their motel rooms and didn't mind eating Christmas dinner in a restaurant.

"Merry Christmas, Reverend. Oh, Ted, look at the snow; it's so, so, New England."

"C'mon, let's get back to the motel and change. I can't wait to hit the slopes."

"Ted, it's Christmas."

"And this," said Ted, "is my Christmas present."

"It was a nice sermon, Reverend," said Ted's wife.

"A little weird," said Ted. His wife elbowed him. "But nice. A change from the usual theme of salvation."

Reverend Swan said, "Salvation is a timeless and universal theme."

Ted nodded. "You said it, Reverend. They had taxes and we have taxes; they had no room in the inn and we have no room in the inn. You couldn't rent a closet on the mountain today."

"The miracle of snowmaking machines," said Reverend Swan.

"That's right, Reverend."

After Reverend Swan removed his vestments and carefully hung them away in their proper place, he joined his wife. As usual, she waited for him in the vestibule. He kissed her on the cheek and wished her a holy Christmas. Together they locked the door and climbed into the ice cube tray. Reverend Swan drove slowly home, past children sliding on the sidewalks.

The church was situated at the head of Main Street (Highway 100 on the state map). Entering the town from the south, the road aimed straight for the church, then curved sharply ninety degrees, in front of Our Lady, and headed up the mountain. The first thing anyone entering Round Corners saw was the church with its white steeple. The rest of the town seemed to huddle around the church in picture postcard perfection, just like a Maud Calhoun original sold at the cash register of the Round Corners Restaurant. Barns, mountains, cows. And churches. The tourists loved them.

When the Swans arrived home, Mrs. Swan made hot chocolate. Their Christmas tradition. Hot chocolate and croissant rolls. "It makes me feel so continental," Mrs. Swan confessed. The Swans sipped hot chocolate in a warm kitchen, their drinks so full of marshmallows they left white mustaches on the Swans's upper lips.

Reverend Swan did not remember driving home in the cold car (apparently his vision had returned) or shaking hands with his parishioners on the steps in nothing but his vestments or Mrs. Swan cutting the greetings short and rushing him back into the church to change into warm clothes.

"You were wonderful today," said Mrs. Swan.

"Really?"

His wife nodded.

"What did I say? I can't remember."

"You were inspirational, as you always are."

"I thought the people seemed a bit restless, bored perhaps."

"Never bored. I'm sure you raised the consciousness of peace and love another notch today."

"Let's hope they remember it later when they run into each other on the slopes."

Mrs. Swan suggested he lie down and rest for a while. She said that often now.

"I *am* tired."

"It's no wonder, making up an entire sermon off the top of your head."

"Did I do that?"

"Yes."

"I didn't give the sermon I wrote on Wednesday?"

"You can save it. Give it another time. A good sermon never grows stale."

"I suppose not."

Reverend Swan slowly ascended the stairs, a white marshmallow mustache still on his face. After every service, Reverend Swan retired to his study. There he grabbed his saxophone, like a desperate smoker scrabbles for a cigarette, and played jazz. The most nonsensical music he could wail. As the notes sailed from the horn, the tension flowed from him, his stomach settled, his life returned to an even keel. And as usual, after a while, Reverend Swan began to think giving sermons wasn't so bad and telling people what's the right thing to do wasn't so difficult.

Automatically, Reverend Swan turned in the direction of the study and the saxophone stand in the corner. Then he remembered there was no saxophone. His wife mentioned driving into Burlington to a pawnshop. She'd seen a saxophone in the window just last week. It probably could be had for a reasonable price. Maybe after Christmas, Reverend Swan said. Right now his heart wasn't in it. Right now he just wanted to lie down in his quiet bedroom.

16

Throwing Snowballs
at the Status Quo

The only plant in Wynn's Cut and Curl is a plastic potted palm.
An artificial palm needs no water or sun or love. People don't
feel compelled to talk to a plastic plant, the way they might
converse with a plant coursing with chlorophyll, a plant they
expect to grow and propagate. You could subject a plastic palm
to loud rock music, freezing temperatures, and cigarette burns all
day long, and not evoke a single response. It shows no stress and
no happiness. It just is.

"I feel like that damn plant," said Wynn Winchester. "A preg-
nant plastic palm. Harvey says I look beautiful. But what does
Harvey know? I'm tired, too tired to do my own hair, after doing
other women's all day. Too tired to sew baby clothes, clean the
house, cook. Harvey practically lives on canned spaghetti.
Freda, do you ever feed your family that spaghetti in a can?"

"The kids love the pasta shaped like the alphabet, but Lewis
goes after the stuff that looks like space monsters. I'd rather eat
turpentine sandwiches myself."

Wynn wrapped the last of Freda's hair around a pink roller.
Thirty rollers, thirty pelvic squeezes. Two weeks ago, she and
Harvey started Lamaze classes. They saw a film of a baby being
born, which Harvey considered a blockbuster. He hightailed it to
the library the next day and checked out more books on child-
birth.

"Harvey's a fount of advice," I said, leaning back in one of the
dryer chairs. The bubble was pushed up. I flipped through one of
Wynn's magazines, looking for tips on keeping your sex life
alive.

Wynn snorted. "He monitors my milk intake. He counts how many cookies I eat. Every time I turn around he's begging me to pant in his face. And some days I just don't feel like it. I bet those other women in Lamaze class practice panting every chance they get. They're going to breeze through childbirth like a mother cat having kittens and pop right back into size nine pants. I'm going to be screaming at Harvey and hyperventilating. And the child will be in college before I ever see the narrow side of a size twelve." Wynn sighed. "Freda, was Lewis with you when you had your babies?"

"Every one. They couldn't keep him out of the delivery room. Lewis was birthing babies with me long before it was the fashionable thing to do. He held my hand, talked to me, wiped the sweat from my face while the other fathers wore the linoleum off the waiting room floor. There isn't a man on earth I'd rather have a baby with than Lewis."

"But when you were pregnant, didn't Lewis drive you crazy with his helpfulness? Didn't you ever want to tell him to leave you alone?"

I looked up and saw a shadow drift across Freda's face.

"I've *never* wanted Lewis to leave me alone. Some men thoroughly enjoy fatherhood. I'd rather have one who cares too much than one who doesn't care at all. They had to drag my daddy out of a bar every time my mother was ready to have a baby. She had to drive *him* to the hospital. It's a time to share, my mother said; you want someone around even if he is half drunk and pukes all over the nurses' station."

Wynn moved Freda to the dryer next to me, flipped the bubble down over Freda's head, and twisted the temperature setting. She knocked on the plastic bubble.

"You all right in there?" Wynn yelled.

Freda gave the thumbs-up sign.

It was a Saturday morning. Freda dragged me out of bed to lend moral support while she sat under a dryer burning her ears in Round Corners's only beauty shop. Under the big bubble dryer, a tiny hurricane whirled around her head, blocking out sound, letting in only thoughts. As Freda thumbed through a magazine, I knew her mind was not on the European chocolate-lovers diet (eat all you want and lose beaucoup pounds a week) or seven ways to develop assertiveness. She even passed on an interview with Cynthia Sands, "the diva of afternoon soap operas."

"Perhaps it's good that Lewis and I are through with having babies," she said in the car on the way to Wynn's. "He's hardly ever around anymore. And I couldn't bear to go through it without him."

That morning she walked into Wynn's shop and said, "Make me into a new woman." She didn't have an appointment. She didn't tell Lewis where she was going. She wanted a new look to lure back her old Lewis Lee, she said.

"I miss that man. I miss those afternoons, when the children were in school and we could take our time loving." The cavorting in those television beds was nothing compared to what hap-pened between her and Lewis, she said. And afterward, he would hold her and they would talk as friends do. "None of that cigarette-after-it's-done shit like they do on television, Maud," Freda said.

Freda's new look resembled many of the new looks walking around Round Corners. Not quite right. Was it lopsided? Maybe the curl was too tight or the cut too short? There was nothing to pile on top of her head as was Freda's style for years. Wynn said she thought the short, earlobe-length hairdo, fluffed out by a perm, was flattering. She showed Freda all kinds of things she could do with two little barrettes. Wynn clipped the curls back from Freda's face.

Later, at the Round Corners Restaurant, I said, "Don't worry, it'll grow out."

"That's something to look forward to," said Freda. "Unless Wynn mistakenly used some solution that stunts growth. I wouldn't be surprised. Her concentration is shot to hell. There are some definite disadvantages to being a one-beautician town." Freda tried combing her hair again. "Oh, what is Lewis going to say?"

"He's going to say you're beautiful."

Freda looked skeptical.

"Really. It kind of grows on you."

"Really?" said Freda, stretching up on her tiptoes to examine her hair in the mirror of the old medicine cabinet hung high over the potatoes in the back room of the Round Corners Restaurant. Freda had to juggle on a sack of Maine's finest spuds to see.

"Really,"

I said, patting Freda's arm.

I flexed my tired shoulders as I passed through the kitchen, grabbing a cheeseburger deluxe for Amos. I hadn't read a newspaper in weeks. I worked and painted, painted and worked, sometimes I ate, sometimes I slept.

Thomas was my clock, making sure I arrived at the restaurant on time and remembered dental appointments and paid the electricity bill. The arrangement was good for the painting, but lousy for my knowledge of world affairs. Amos and Bartholomew did their best to keep me informed on current events. It was risky, relying on them for my sole contact with the outside world. They viewed life through a different window than most people, one of those windows common to New England houses, a little window stuck on its side under the eaves. The window was skewed, and you tended to slant your head when you peered through it. To Amos and Bartholomew, nothing was as bad as it could be, but then everything was damn near awful. They loved to consider the worst that could happen and then elaborate on it.

"I knew they were going to sink that boat," said Amos.

"Me, too," said Bartholomew.

"What?" I said, placing the cheeseburger deluxe in front of Amos and refilling his coffee cup.

"The cruise ship," said Amos. "Those astronomers are pointing out the stars to Davey Jones now."

"That's a fact," said Bartholomew. "Sunk it just like they said they would."

"Oh, no," I said.

"You just can't deal with people who have suicide as a career goal," said Amos.

"You don't have anything to bargain with," said Bartholomew, nodding. "Human life is about the same as an ant's."

"Poor Thomas," I said.

"Thomas?"

"He's partial to astronomers."

"We're all partial to something," said Bartholomew.

"Exactly," said Amos. "Those people who took that ship were nuts, not dumb. You think they picked the world's top scientists out of a hat? They knew how important those astronomers were to the world and what would happen if they were blown off the planet. We're going to have to live on those damn stars some day, and now who's going to tell us how to do it?"

"None of them survived?"

"Maybe the ones who knew how to swim and still had arms and legs to do it with," said Amos. "Must have looked like some kind of war zone."

"And don't forget the sharks," said Bartholomew.

"Must have been terrible," said Amos.

"That's a fact," I said.

I had to find Thomas. Freda, not eager to go home until she had fooled with her hair some more, agreed to close up the restaurant. When I arrived home, the yellow van was parked in the drive. I started calling Thomas's name the moment I stepped through the door. I searched every room of the house. The radio was playing a country song in the kitchen. The dishes were washed. Thomas was a better housekeeper in despair than I am in contentment. Upstairs the bedrooms were empty. My bed was made. I never made my bed. A stack of freshly laundered clothes had been placed neatly on the corner. The attic was dark. No one answered my calls. The emptiness frightened me.

I jumped when the phone rang. It was T-Bone.

"He's over here. I pumped him full of Rolling Rocks. He's got the tolerance of a baby."

"Thanks."

"You coming to get him?"

"Can I just stay at your place, too?"
"What am I running? A hotel?"

Lines. Shapes. Line becomes shape. Shape becomes form.
Form becomes content.

Feather the line, coax it across the page, into a circle, into a
leg, into a backbone. Go back and give it strength. Dark. Darker.
Strong enough to stand up to your moods and emotions and
opinions.

In the painting, the sun is shining from the east. It makes
shade. Rub. Smear. Shade. Suddenly, there is roundness and
volume.

There is depth, thanks to cosmology and a charcoal pencil.

Where is perspective? More line. More shape. More form.

*I can't draw fast enough, George. It's wonderful. I feel
flow.*

The switch has been flipped, at last.

My God, George, I feel . . .

Line becomes shape. Shape becomes form. Form becomes
content.

Content becomes . . . content becomes . . .

A cow.

This painting is getting bigger every day. At its current rate of
growth, it will burst the seams of the studio, and then I'll really
have a mess.

The painting has grown into an ill-mannered child. It devours
gallons of paint, burps outrageously, and asks what's next. Like
all mothers forced to live with their children for days and nights
without end, I am a woman on the edge. I can't stand it any
longer. I have to talk to someone. Preferably an adult.

What can I do, George?

*Relax? That's it? I expected more from a man with cosmic
experience.*

Nothing about the painting was working. "What can I do?" I

asked Thomas.

"Read a book," suggested Thomas. "Take your mind off your problems."

Thomas reads the strangest books in the world. He lent me a collection of "scientific/realistic/metaphysic" essays called *Maintenance of the Universe*. The essays are written from the point of view of a man who describes himself as "janitor to the stars."

"How do you paint a comet?" asks the author of *Maintenance of the Universe*. "Do you climb to the top of the world's tallest ladder and hold out the brush as it streaks by? Do you sail to a satellite, wait, and fling the whole can of paint on it as it passes? Or do you turn the binoculars on yourself and look far away to that place inside of you that is too deep to swim to and too quick to catch, to that place where you can change the color of a comet just by wishing it so?

"Such are the considerations of the celestial handyman."

I threw down my paintbrush, swung around and searched the shelf of paint cans, selected six, and packed them in a box along with several brushes and a roll of paper towels. I cut off the tips of my woolen gloves and pulled on a coat.

Outside I stared at the side of the barn and the faded painting of Milky Way. For a moment, I heard my father again the day he walked into the mural on a barn door. I heard him howling and saw him holding his nose as it turned red and tender and twice its size. And I remembered how he held out his arms, when he was sure he'd smell again, and we collapsed against each other. I felt our chests rising and falling with our giggles. I tasted the cool, foggy morning, as we sucked the mist from each other's mouths.

I shoveled a path to the painting, propped the box of paints in the snowbank, and set to work. George said Milky Way's big black-and-white holstein body reminded him of inkblots. I tried to ignore him. He began to pitch a softball against the side of the barn. *Bang, bang, bang.*

All right, George, inkblots. Bang, bang. *What do I see in this one? A butterfly? What do you mean, in winter?*

Bang, bang.

*A lion in a dentist's chair. Is this painful for me? Who are
you, Freud?*

Bang.

*A wing walker riding a pterodactyl. Is the wing walker
frightened? No. He's happy. At last he's flying.*

Bang.

*I think that is all the time we have today, Mrs. Calhoun?
Cute, George, real cute.*

Thomas drove home that evening the way one does with his
eyes on paintings and not paths—into a snowbank. He didn't
stop to consider any damage to the van, he was so excited about
Milky Way. He rushed to get out of the vehicle, flinging open the
van door, which struck the snowbank and bounced back into
Thomas's nose. He entered the studio cursing and holding the
injured extremity.

"What the hell is going on, Maud?"

"Going on? Nothing. You better put an ice bag on that nose."

The next morning, Thomas called T-Bone, who arrived in a
truck with a big winch, and together they pulled the yellow van
out of the snowbank. It took two seconds. The day was bright as
a beach, the sun reflecting off the snow. Twenty-five degrees and
sunny. Vermonters considered such days a gift, a picnic, a won-
derful surprise like finding a ten dollar bill tucked between the
pages of a book you hadn't picked up in years.

The two banged into the house, knocking the snow from their
boots, unzipping jackets, and tossing them on pegs by the door.
"It feels good in here," Thomas said, heading for the shelf where
the coffee was stored and expertly filling the coffeemaker.
Thomas the California boy wasn't sold on winter yet. The sun
coming in the kitchen window beamed down motes into the air.
It flowed over Thomas's head and shoulder, and suddenly he was
a golden child. He turned, smiled, shoved a lock of golden hair
from his eyes, and leaned against the counter.

I fiddled with a pencil, doodling on the red-checkered tablecloth Thomas had bought to set the atmosphere for his last Italian dinner. I heard T-Bone gasp and quickly looked at him. He stared at my doodling. I glanced down at the drawing. It was Thomas the golden child, bathed in light, in peace.

T-Bone nearly lost three holsteins in January. The narrow escapes threw T-Bone off balance. He felt himself teetering horribly. It frightened him. "The only place I feel safe is in your arms," he said.

But I was painting again. He knew what that meant: Sometimes I worked through the night. I forgot to eat and bathe and call him when I wasn't going to be over. "I used to be able to take it, Maud," he said one night, holding me tightly, under the covers in his big bed. "It used to be enough to just watch over you. Now I need more. God, I think I'm turning into George."

T-Bone the worrier sat at my kitchen table, studying a coffee mug. None of my dishes match. I do not think in terms of eight-piece place settings. If I see a piece of pottery I like, I buy it. That's that. No wondering if it will complement the rest of my china. "Has this pottery been tested for lead paint?" T-Bone asked.

Such potential failures as not saving me from lead poisoning prey on T-Bone's mind constantly now. Suppose there was a blizzard and it piled up snow for a week and I couldn't get out for food or wood. He was sure his truck wouldn't start. He would try to limp the mile between our doors, but all the landmarks would be buried, and he would wander in circles until spring. By then, I could be dead from starvation or frozen or moved away. Such was T-Bone's luck.

Or suppose the government needed him for a top secret mission. They required a man of his skills: a man fluent in two languages, good with animals, able to keep a secret, not too talkative, walks with a limp. They want him to impersonate an old sea captain who has retired with his pet parrot to the Vermont hills, but reportedly still is active in the smuggling business. The deal goes down on a boat on Lake Champlain, but promptly is blown by T-Bone the valiant sea captain with a weak stomach. T-Bone forgot to tell the government men he hates boats.

"I hate change," T-Bone said, sipping his coffee. He shook his head. So many things in T-Bone's world seemed to be changing. He had no confidence in himself or his ability to keep his herd healthy. Was it his imagination or were the women of Round Corners wearing their hair wilder? He thought he saw the librarian in a punk cut yesterday. That same day he passed Reverend Swan going into Snowden's and the minister didn't even say hello or bless you when T-Bone sneezed. The least you could expect from a minister is comfort in the time of a cold, T-Bone thought. He remembered when he was a boy and Father Julian held the crossed candles under his throat to bless his tonsils, voice box, and sinuses. The doctor had to remove his tonsils anyway, and no amount of ice cream would restore his faith in God's henchman, Saint Blaise, the great protector of throats.

"Do you want to drive into Burlington and catch a movie tonight?" asked T-Bone, continuing to eye with distrust the suspected carrier of lead poisoning.

"Thanks, but I'm working on the painting tonight. Why don't you ask Thomas?"

T-Bone put the mug down with a thump. "Because it's not as much fun sharing a bucket of popcorn with Thomas."

"You could accomplish some real male bonding," I said. "Digging into the same bucket of buttery, high-cholesterol snacks ought to be right up there with hunting down small defenseless animals together and roasting them on a spit."

"You've been reading those magazines at Wynn's again, haven't you?"

T-Bone coaxed and pressed, and I refused and sent him home to sulk. "Men don't sulk," he said, slamming out of the house. I watched from the kitchen window as the limping T-Bone stalked past the snow cow Thomas made yesterday. The cow wore a toga, a Halley's Comet baseball cap, and a Mona Lisa smile. T-Bone stopped and stared at the pile of snow in the shape of

Plato the Bovine. Suddenly he bent, scooped up a handful of snow, formed a snowball, and hurled it at the cow. "Bond this," he yelled, flattening the cow's snout with a second fast ball. He spun to launch a third attack, lost his balance on a patch of ice, and went down with a crash. When I last saw him, he was rubbing his rump and climbing into his truck.

"Right. Men don't sulk," I said, heading up to the studio. "My ass."

17

Don't Get Your Gooey Fingerprints on My Crystal Ball

The sign said, "Sister Wilma—Spiritual Counselor to the Stars and Skiers." A palm was painted below Sister Wilma's name. An eye winked from the center of the palm. Mountains, presumably Vermont's Green Mountains, were pictured in the background. At the foot of the hills, in precise letters, was: "All Credit Cards Accepted."

Six high-powered floodlights lit both sides of the sign at night. Sister Wilma said hers was a prominent clientele, and that she did most of her business after dark. I believed it. A man practically knocked over Ella as he hurried to leave Sister Wilma's undetected. "Sorry," he grunted, then fled down the steps, his back hunched, his collar turned up, his hat pulled low. We saw him shove a pair of sunglasses on his nose as he climbed into a red sports car and roared away into the night.

"Don't we know him?" Ella said.

"I wonder," said Sister Wilma from behind us, making us jump, "when we will cease to apologize for seeking spirituality in an out-of-the-way place."

We turned and met Sister Wilma, a plain woman who carried forty pounds more than she should on those Earth-shoe-clad feet. ("I didn't know they sold Earth shoes anymore," Ella whispered.) Sister Wilma was dressed like a hausfrau, in polyester pants and striped linen blouse. Her hair was permed against its better judgment. The tight Afro gave her an unnatural appearance, bug-eyed and jowly like a frog in a bathtub. She had porcelain skin, which would never tan in a million years. A million lifetimes.

Sister Wilma said she was an Egyptian slave in one of her former lives, and an Indian princess. I wondered if she had ever met Raj in her Egyptian days. He, too, claimed many pasts and personalities.

We sat in Sister Wilma's living room, in chairs with plaid cushions and chunky armrests. On a table beside Sister Wilma was a Bible, an alarm clock, and a blue jay's feather. All the plants in the room were dead or dying. Sister Wilma asked us if we had ever been to a spiritual counselor before. We said no. Sister Wilma explained that she worked in a state of split consciousness. "I will be talking to you, and you can talk to me."

Sister Wilma glanced at the clock. "Please don't let me run over. Gotta pick up my daughter at nine." Sister Wilma smiled. "Big volleyball game tonight."

We nodded.

Sister Wilma then picked up the blue jay feather, closed her eyes, and began to breathe deeply. The room was silent except for Sister Wilma's breathing, which grew steadily calmer and louder. Although her breathing was controlled, her fingers were not. Nervously, she pulled the feather through her fingers, over and over again.

I poked Ella and pointed toward Sister Wilma. Ella had thirty-five dollars burning inside her pocket. She fingered the bills and wondered how to ask if Sister Wilma knew where her notebook was—the notebook that contained "Howling Mad Home," her poem about Round Corners.

"You know," said Sister Wilma, "I've been doing readings since I was twelve years old, and it never changes. People never change. Take the guy who was in here before you. He wanted me to 'look into the cards' and tell him if his wife knew he was fooling around. People have to have tarot cards and crystal balls and star charts. They want black veils and hoop earrings. I don't even have pierced ears.

"And they think we're all crooked. The first thing they say is, 'Tell me something about myself.' I'm put through more tests in a month than most college students take in a lifetime. I'm supposed to be able to tell them what they had for breakfast this morning and if they'll get a promotion tomorrow. People love to hear what they already know about themselves. If I were paying the kind of money I'm being paid, I'd want to know something I don't know."

Sister Wilma stroked the feather again and again. Her breathing bounced off the silent walls of the room. Ella reached for my hand. I don't know why I agreed to come with her. I didn't believe the Sister Wilmas of the world. But Ella sounded so desperate on the telephone. I squeezed Ella's hand.

"I can't read palms," Sister Wilma went on. " I have no idea what significance the number five has in your life. I can't shuffle a deck of pinochle cards without bending the corners. But people don't want to know. They want to see the crystal ball. For a while, I used one of those dime-store snow scenes in a globe. The customers loved it."

I understood: barns, mountains, cows. The tourists loved them.

"I've been psychic all my life," Sister Wilma said. "I've always known I was different. My father recognized what I was from the start."

"Yes," I said.

"I tried to hide my abilities. I wanted to be like everyone else. Kids can be so cruel, y'know. But Father wouldn't let me. He never let me doubt myself."

"No, he wouldn't," I said.

"He always told me I was born with all I needed to be. You are put on this earth, he said, not to become something new, but to discover how old you are. We already have all the answers inside us." Sister Wilma laughed. "Isn't that a kick in the head? Better not let that get out. I'd be out of business."

The alarm clock jangled. I reached over and turned it off. Slowly, Sister Wilma opened her eyes and smiled. She placed the mangled blue jay feather on the table.

We rose and Ella handed over her thirty-five dollars.

Sister Wilma pocketed the bills, without looking at them, and smiled. "Did I answer all your questions?"

"Yes," I said.

"Good," she said, padding across the floor in her Earth shoes. She grabbed her coat, escorted us to the door, and locked it behind us. As she headed for the blue compact parked beside my van, she chattered, "I hope Lucy got to play. She warms the bench and hopes. The coach says she's too short. Short, I say, look at the Chinese and then talk to me about short volleyball players."

We watched Sister Wilma drive off into the world of high school athletics, then wearily climbed into the van. We drove to my house, cracked open a couple of Rolling Rocks, and put our feet up on the coffee table.

"Well," said Ella.

"Well," I said.

Ella didn't go home that night. Thomas woke us the next morning when he stubbed his toe on a pyramid of beer cans by Ella's leg. Thomas drove Ella into town. She insisted on opening the post office despite a temporary sensitivity to loud sounds and a throbbing head. Neither rain, snow, gloom of night nor Rolling Rocks, apparently, can stop the U.S. mail.

It was about 10:35, while she was pulling several packages from a mailbag, that she heard Frank opening the store next door. She harrumphed; he'd overslept. "What did you do, Frank, *forget* to set the alarm?" she said, sticking out her tongue at the barricade blocking the entrance to the store. The taunt hurt her head and Ella winced. She poured two aspirin from a bottle in the top drawer and chewed them without water. Frank hated when she did that.

Ella returned to the sorting. *Redbook* for Wynn. A farm journal for T-Bone. A letter from Maine for Reverend Swan. A letter for her. Ella stopped, reread the name on the envelope. It *was* addressed to her. She tore open the letter and gasped. It was from the editor of a literary magazine. Ella remembered the editor from the writers conference. She'd purchased one of his magazines, paid by check, and, apparently, was now permanently ensconced on his mailing list. The letter was a form letter, a call for submissions—the first Ella had ever received. Ella screamed with joy and hopped around the post office; letters flurried behind her dancing to the floor. She whirled and whirled until suddenly she realized "Howling Mad Home" was the only poem suitable for such a magazine.

"Oh no," howled Ella, laying her head on the counter among the stamps and sobbing.

Ella's final wail was too much for Frank. He burst through the barricade with a bump and a crash, then had to rest a moment against the doorjamb. "What is it?" he panted. "Ella? Why are you crying?"

Frank's entrance startled Ella. She gaped at him, a line of stamps stuck to her forehead. "I . . ."

"Are you hurt?" Frank asked.

"No, I . . ."

"Then what in the hell are you doing screaming bloody murder and scaring me and where were you last night and . . ."

"I . . ."

"Ella, I was worried sick."

"I didn't think you'd notice."

"Not notice! You didn't come home all night."

"Well, you didn't notice the ham was burned on Christmas."

"I noticed; I was being polite."

"Polite."

Now that he had his breath back after that heroic rescue, Frank pushed away from the door and took Ella in his arms. He gently peeled off the stamps from her forehead. She clung to him and thought how good he smelled.

"Now tell me what this is all about," he said.

Ella handed him the letter. Frank read it.

"Tonight we'll look for that notebook," he said. "We'll turn the house, the post office, even the store upside down."

"But tonight you have barbershop quartet practice."

"So. I can miss it once."

"You never miss."

Frank shrugged.

Ella snuggled closer. "You sure came through that door fast."

"I should have hurdled the snowbank. I tripped over a case of beans. My shin hurts like hell."

"Oh dear." They looked at the mess of boxes and cans and rolls of toilet paper.

"C'mon," he said. "I'll fix you a cup of coffee, and you can sit by the stove. I think I even have a bear claw left from breakfast."

That night Frank and Ella did search and search and search. At 4:05 in the morning, a whoop of glee nearly woke up Round Corners, and if anyone had peeked inside the front window of Snowden's General Store, they would have seen Ella Snowden dancing around the canned goods hugging her notebook.

They found the notebook as they dismantled the barricade; it was in a box marked "pastry." Ella remembers it all now. She remembers working on her poem late one night at the post office and being attacked by the munchies, as they called it at the writers conference. Overcome by a yearning for something sweet, she let herself into the store to sneak two packages of bear claws from the box marked "pastry."

"I must have left the notebook on the box, and it got knocked inside by accident," Ella said. "I remember standing beside the box and stuffing my face with bear claws and then walking right out the door, locking up, and driving home."

Ella made a believer of me. Sister Wilma was right. The answers are inside us. Sometimes right in our digestive track.

18

Looking for Life's Rest Stops

I love the smell of cinnamon rolls. Oh, that's right, you can't smell them, can you, George? What a shame.

I don't recall you baking cinnamon rolls like these, so full of butter and cinnamon. To be frank, George, your swirls were always crooked. Thomas has a way of rolling the dough, the layers of butter and cinnamon sugar so perfect, never crooked . . . and the way he seals the long rolls of dough with just the proper pinch. Sorry, George, but you never had the pinching touch.

Pinching, not pinch hitting.

What do they taste like? Melt-in-your-mouth ecstasy, that's all. It's like your insides really can't believe how good they are. Of course, you wouldn't understand; you don't have insides.

That was rotten—teasing George. I know. Corporeal comedy. I really can't defend myself. It *is* like shooting fish in a barrel. What can I say? Someone reload my gun. I get this way when the Good Cheer Lady bit is forced upon me. I explained it all to Thomas as he shoved a list of deliveries in my hand. I have a lousy bedside manner. "Good thing none of these people are bedridden then," said an unsympathetic Thomas.

I was shanghaied into delivering the cinnamon rolls because Thomas refused to leave his yeast. Yeast, according to Thomas, was a temperamental ingredient. And so it didn't hurt to talk to it occasionally like a yucca plant or a philodendron. Thomas found nothing unusual in discoursing at length with fermenting fungi.

"It's part of the plant kingdom," he said.

Somewhere in Thomas's past, cinnamon rolls came to be the universal comfort food. It was Thomas's solution to unhappiness. He baked enough cinnamon rolls to force the entire town of Round Corners onto a diet. He was optimistic that the cinnamon rolls would work. I wasn't sure how flour, sugar, butter, cinnamon, and yeast was supposed to snap Reverend Swan out of the doldrums or give Ella back her illusions.

Ella peeked inside the tin and began to cry. She said to thank Thomas, but "Cinnamon rolls aren't bear claws." When Ella reread "Howling Mad Home," she discovered it wasn't nearly as good as she remembered. In fact, it sucked like a vacuum cleaner. Personally, I don't think that's all bad. If we all wrote perfect poems the first time, revision wouldn't exist; second chance would never have been born. And then where is the learning in that?

I'm sure Sister Wilma would say Ella once wrote a perfect poem—in a former life—and now all she had to do was remember how she did it. It was just as Ella thought: Memory (or the lack thereof) was the bane of her life.

Perhaps memory, not comets, is the stuff of life. It, too, visits us in fleeting moments, leaving sparks of recognition, embers that might have told us something if only we had paid attention to them instead of shoving them aside and saying, "I'll think about that later—right now, I have to worry about what to cook for dinner or how Junior's going to get through college or whether there will be Social Security when I'm old."

I eased my foot from the accelerator, switched on Catfish Joe's noonday show, grabbed a gooey cinnamon roll with my mittened hand, and took my time arriving at Reverend Swan's house. This good neighbor stuff was not all it was cracked up to be; in fact, I found it downright dangerous. T-Bone threw his cinnamon rolls at my head. "Tell that kid he can keep his damn bread. He probably forgot the raisins anyway."

Thomas's good cheer offering sent Wynn into another bout of depression. "Great. More calories. He must be in league with Junior," Wynn said, passing them around to her clients.

I was apprehensive about my reception at the Swan house. However, that day I was in luck. Reverend Swan was shoveling the sidewalk. He loves shoveling snow. He prays while he fights the white stuff, his prayers taking on the rhythm of his work. *Scoop/swing/pitch. Scoop/swing/pitch. Lord/I am/but a man. Lost/and/alone. Have mercy/on/my soul.*

I can dig that, not the praying part, but the shoveling. The solace of physical labor, T-Bone calls it. Sounds rather whimsical for T-Bone. But snow does that to you. It turns us all into blithering poets, cowboy romantics, muscle-bound maniacs. The snow war is an honorable battle. The shovel a noble weapon. The ache in the small of the back from bending and flinging a courageous casualty. When I was painting, back in the pre-George period, and I got stuck, I'd shovel snow. In the cold quiet of swinging shovel, I cleared my head as I cleared the path, made my mind as blank as the snow. And answers would come to me. Some winters, when questions fell faster than snow and there wasn't a flake left on the sidewalks and paths, I shoveled the fields. There were paths, thoroughfares, avenues all over our farm for the cows and the cats and the rabbits.

Reverend Swan attacked the snow with a vengeance. Apparently, he had a lot on his mind. Mrs. Swan thought he should hire a boy to do the shoveling. "You're sixty years old," she said. When he shoveled, she ran back and forth from whatever work she was doing—ironing, baking, sewing—to the front window. She expected to see him prostrate in the snowbank someday, his heart refusing to lift one more flake.

Hire a boy, she said. Just like the one he had once been in a little town on the New Hampshire–Vermont border. Back then, he shoveled snow to earn money. He bought his first football with snow money, and a scarf for his father, and a new rosary for his mother. It was her birthday. The students at the seminary outside of town made religious articles—rosaries, prayer books, medals, statues for the dashboard—in a manufacturing plant, where they also learned to be priests. For his mother, he chose a rosary with blue beads, and inside every bead was a picture of the

Virgin Mary. Never had he seen a rosary so beautiful. He asked the seminarian at the cash register to bless it for him. His mother insisted on having the blessing redone by a "real" priest after mass on Sunday.

Those beads had come in handy in the following years. He grew up, planned to become a priest/rosary maker, met Mrs. Swan, fell in love, married, and "deserted the church," as his mother put it. When he became a minister in "that heathen faith," his mother told him, she prayed for him on her special Virgin Mary rosary. When she died, the undertaker entwined the blue beads about her fingers. They were entombed with her, much as horses and slaves were buried with pharaohs. She would need them in the next world, apparently, to pray for her wayward Episcopalian son.

There was another thing Reverend Swan bought with snow money. Music lessons. His mother never understood the saxophone. She wanted him to take organ lessons, then he could play at mass. And perhaps, if he had studied the organ as she wanted, he'd still be Catholic today.

For it is from the saxophone that he first learned doubt. Limits, the saxophone said, can be broken. It does not have to be as it always was. You can be free, the saxophone said. You can fly. And it came to be that the saxophone was his belief, that God lived in its clear notes, not in some glass beads.

I stood on top of a frozen snowbank, towering above Reverend Swan, as he finished the end of the sidewalk. Finally he leaned on the shovel and squinted up at me.

"Maud, I have to confess to feeling out of touch with God lately."

He thought I might understand, it being an artist thing. Ever since Odie flattened his saxophone, Reverend Swan had been praying, frantically, all the time, everywhere, in hopes of regaining his former spiritual status. He prayed so he wouldn't think. He repeated prayers from the Catholic missal he had memorized as a child. If he had known Arabic, he would have quoted the Koran. If he had known Hebrew, he would have recited the

Torah. Anything to keep his mind from working—alphabetizing, editing, correcting, arranging his being.

At night was the worst time. When he slept, he could not pray, and then his subconscious ran amok. Often he struggled awake in the darkness, sweating, gasping, thinking. And the thought he awoke with was always the same: "What if we really are all alone, and there is no one else out there; what if there never was anyone here but us, and when we go—we're gone?" Reverend Swan was utterly shocked by the blasphemous train his thoughts had hopped.

Obviously, Reverend Swan needed a Rolling Rock, but today I was without my supplies. I shoved the cinnamon rolls under his nose. "I know what you mean. The feeling of purposelessness can drive you crazy. Cinnamon roll?"

Reverend Swan tugged off a glove and reached for a roll. "I can't accept the concept of purposelessness," Reverend Swan said. "We are more important than a particle of space dust. I'd rather become a Hindu and look forward to a life as a worm or a cow than accept that it was all for naught." Reverend Swan paused in midchew. "A Hindu! Mother would blister her fingers on the beads."

I am the resident chief of self-doubt; everyone knows it, and so, whenever they're feeling even the slightest bit diffident, they come to me, Mother Cowboy Confessor. My advice is as deep as one of Catfish Joe's Top Ten.

"You can't travel through life if you think someone has gone ahead of you and removed all the rest stops," I said.

"It seems such a cruel trick to play: To make a man a minister and not give him the skills to attend to his people's needs. Why would God do that? Why don't I know the answers? Could it be because there are no answers?"

Mrs. Swan stuck her head out the door. "You should hire a boy to do that. Are you two going to eat all those cinnamon rolls yourself?"

Reverend Swan sighed and rammed his shovel into a mountainous bank near the door. It was ready for him there, when the next storm blew through, or he needed to find some answers.

The smell of chocolate and marshmallows met us as we clomped into the house. Reverend Swan shrugged off his coat and bent to slip off his boots. When he straightened, his wife stood in front of him holding out a steaming cup. He took it and she kissed him, saying she had some ironing to do. She grabbed a cinnamon roll on her way out of the room.

We eased into chairs at the kitchen table. I chased the marshmallows in my hot chocolate with a spoon while Reverend Swan glanced through the mail. Utility bill, as usual, higher than the month before. Reminder from the diocesan office in Burlington of the annual spring meeting and bake sale. Flyer from a chain of hardware stores: "Fix up, clean up, spruce up for spring."

And a letter from Brunswick, Maine.

Reverend Swan didn't know anyone in Brunswick, Maine. Almost cautiously, he slit the envelope and read it.

Slowly his hand began to tremble.

Startled, I grabbed his wrist and whispered his name. "Are you all right? Reverend, is it your heart?"

He shook his head, opened his mouth, closed it. He handed the letter to me. "Read it aloud," he croaked.

Dear Reverend Swan,

You probably don't remember me . . .

I glanced at the bottom of the page. Walter Lamb. It wasn't a name I recognized.

We came through your way last fall, me and the kids.

The Mainiacs. It's difficult to forget ten kids.

You put us up for the night, and the next morning your good wife cooked us breakfast. When we left your house, we drove on to the address you gave us and your friend there, Reverend Douglass, said he heard the paper mill near Brunswick was hiring. So we drove to Brunswick. And what do you know, by nightfall I had a job. A man at the mill had an uncle who had a cheap apartment to let. It was small, but the kids got to like sleeping on the floor when we were at your place. Your missus told 'em that's the way the Chinese sleep, and they didn't mind being Chinese for a while.

Work at the mill ain't nothing like work on the farm. Don't know if I'll ever get used to working with a roof over my head. The noise of the machines is louder than I ever thought sound could be. It's nothing like the quiet fields. And beans sure smell sweeter than pulp. But me and the kids decided we could save a little money here. Maybe buy a few acres out of town. I don't know about growing beans in this sandy Maine soil, but if anyone can do it, I can.

The kids are doin' fine. They're all in school. They really like Maine. They like the beach the best. None of us had ever seen the ocean before. The little ones ran right to the edge the first time we saw it, stuck their fingers in it, and ran back. "It's so cold," they said. We just stood there in the wind and watched it for the longest time. No one said a word. Finally, Sally said, "Papa, ain't it ever gonna stop?" We all laughed.

"Darlin'," I said, "it'll last longer than all of us."

"Doesn't it ever get tired?" Sally asked.

"No," I said, "never."

When I look at the ocean, I think about you, Reverend. I think about what you said about never giving up because I had something to give. Keep going, you said, for the kids. That night after the kids were asleep, I never talked so much before about anything, much less my wife and the farm. But you let me talk. Even after I told you I wasn't Episcopalian.

You said in this life there was no coincidences. You said I was meant to take those kids and make a new home for them. I don't think about my wife much anymore, or the way she left us. I think about my kids and the farm we're going to have someday. I want it to look out on the ocean. Because when I look at the ocean, it gives me the strength to never stop. Just like you did.

The letter was signed, *Walter Lamb.*

We sat in the silence left by Walter Lamb's words. Moments slipped away loudly on the old clock on the wall; the cuckoo bird popped out, just as a jay fluttered to the snowbank outside and squawked. Slowly, ever so slowly, Reverend Swan's lips curved into a smile.

I handed the letter back to him. "It seems you make a pretty good rest stop. I think I'll send you all my referrals from now on."

19

They Come and They Go

Perhaps every town has its dreams.

Just as people do.

Some towns want to grow and grow, big enough to attract a McDonald's, a Pizza Hut, a Kentucky Fried Chicken. They stretch eagerly toward the interstate highway over the hill and the travelers who need to eat and sleep and use the rest room. A four-lane strip of road and an off-ramp can be a town's ticket to life. Life in the fast food lane.

Other places don't mind being small. They take pride in the fact that nothing has changed since their forefathers bought the land for a bead and a prayer. They're not afraid to take on the government. To say, "You're durn tootin'," when the Postal Service asks if they *really* need a post office. To say, "No, thank you," to federal authorities waving emergency funds for snow removal under their noses. "We're perfectly capable of clearing our own snow, thank you. There was snow before there was matching grants."

Such is Round Corners.

If Round Corners has a dream, it is one of balance, of not letting the government push it one way and the outsiders push it another. The countryside is speckled with New York stockbrokers raising sheep, corporate vice presidents running businesses by modem, and best-selling authors hunched over woodstoves. They come to Vermont to get away. They want out of the rat race and into nature. They want to live off the land in L.L. Bean boots and cashmere sweaters. They seek self-sufficiency. They write Christmas cards to city friends: "No traffic, no rush, no ulcers, no muggings. Yes, paradise. Am sending under separate cover can of maple syrup I made from sap from my own trees. May your holidays be simple and happy." The imprint on the back of the card is a designer line of stationery sold only in the most exclusive shops in New York.

They come to escape and end up trying to turn the town into the one they left. They have all kinds of ideas for streetlights and road maintenance. They grow impatient when voters turn down a bond issue to renovate the seventy-four-year-old school but support an initiative declaring the town "nuclear free." ("How many ships armed with nuclear weapons do we get in Round Corners?" said Sheriff Odie Dorfmann, who opposed the proposal on grounds of absurdity.)

And then there are those who come, never intending to change anything, and throw our lives up into the air like a basket of colored balls. When we land, we are mixed up, out of place, looking at things differently, and likely to never be the same again.

Thomas tossed the sleeping bag into the back of the yellow van. Again, he surveyed the contents of the van. Again, I asked if he had the computer.

Yes.

And the modem? Yes. The binoculars? Yes. Star charts? Yes.

"Did you fold and pack the clothes that were in the dryer?"

"Yes, and I even folded yours; they're on your bed."

Thomas was leaving. He had a ticket for Australia in his pocket. An airplane ticket. He could have gone by boat, but after the sinking of the Star in Heaven, the astronomers' cruise ship, I wasn't keen on the idea of Thomas traveling by boat. "I'll worry until you dock in Sydney. I'll probably need dental work from grinding my teeth. I'll develop a twitch. I won't get a thing done."

T-Bone augmented my arguments with a grisly description of seasickness, which made Thomas's face turn the color of my van just thinking about it.

"All right," he said, "the friendly skies it is."

That was just a week ago, and now he was going. Australia. The southern hemisphere has a whole different sky of stars this time of year, Thomas said, and besides, it's warmer there. This is summer in Australia.

T-Bone handed Thomas a duffel bag, the last item to be stowed in the van. Thomas carelessly flung it in and turned toward us. "I hate this," he said. "My mom says departures are tough because luggage reminds people that it's too late to say all the things they had wanted to say. So they babble inane, stupid stuff." He grabbed my hand. "Let's not be inane and stupid. Quick, let's discuss the meaning of life, why we're here, where we came from. Anything. A joke. Something that we'll remember for the rest of our lives."

I smiled and placed my hand on his cheek, knowing that although he spoke with a teasing voice, Thomas in some small place in his heart really meant it. I wanted to give him that, some profound sentiment to send him off into the sunset. But I couldn't think of a single thing to say, not even some country-and-western song wisdom. Somehow I knew he'd be all right. I told him once he had the gift of fitting in anywhere, that he was one of those people who created their own opportunities. Finally, I think, he believed me.

I hugged him. He sighed and swallowed; so did I. Finally, sniffing, I pushed away.

"I'll send you photos. Pictures of me in a bush hat. Of kangaroos."

I smiled shakily.

Again, Thomas checked the van: sleeping bag, duffel bag, computer, binoculars, cassette player, painting. It was a self-portrait. The first one I'd ever tried. It was small, the right size for a traveling man, just as he requested. In the painting, I'm hugging Milky Way. Both of us are wearing big smiles. The cow's bridgework looks like something out of an editorial cartoon of Jimmy Carter.

Thomas studied the pile. His worldly possessions were exactly as he had left them. Nothing had jumped out of the van while his back was turned. He would not have to go through the indignity of dragging a duffel bag, kicking and screaming, back to the van or bribing a computer cable into behaving with a call to the local bulletin board. He couldn't put it off any longer.

He turned and shook hands with T-Bone, the man who'd taught him everything he'd ever need to know about the end of a cow, and then some.

"Take care of yourself," T-Bone said.

"Take care of her," Thomas said nodding toward me.

"Go," I said, pulling his head down and kissing his cheek.

Thomas nodded again, then climbed into the van. It started on the fourth attempt. Then, with a grin and a wave, he was off, a bright yellow dot buzzing down the snow-packed road. We stood in the cold, shivering, watching the yellow van out of sight. A junco in the maple overhead chirped. T-Bone stamped his feet.

"He's smart to get out before the thaw."

"Yes," I said. "Mud season does crazy things to a person."

Harvey Winchester finally called at seven.

"Where are you?" Wynn cried.

"Still at work," he said. The last real snowstorm of the season, the last humdinger, had downed trees, which in turn had dropped power lines. "There's not a lick of light on the whole campus. We've got to remove those trees so the linemen can get to work. Every building, including the dormitories, is pitch dark. Who knows what those kids are up to?"

"Probably trying to stay warm," Wynn said.

"That's what I'm afraid of," Harvey said.

"But what about the Lamaze class tonight?"

"Go ahead without me," Harvey said. "And take notes."

Wynn hung up on her husband and headed for the Round Corners Restaurant. There she whined over her second piece of German chocolate cake, "*He* was the one who liked going to classes. *I* only put up with all that panting nonsense for him. And now *he's* out in the cold coaching linemen instead of me. This is the rehearsal of the birth of his own child, for gawdsake."

The clock said 7:17. Even if he left that very minute, Harvey wouldn't make it on time. The small college was a twenty-mile drive, and tonight the road was swarming with snowplows. Wynn jammed her arms into Harvey's big, old down parka. She couldn't zip hers anymore. Harvey's parka was too old, too worn even for Harvey, a fashion illiterate if there ever was one. He offered to buy Wynn a new coat. But she said, don't waste the money. She didn't care how she looked. She glanced at her reflection in the window. She looked like shit in hunter green.

She squared her shoulders the way martyrs of all time have prepared themselves. I took one look at her face and relented. "All right, I'll coach you tonight. So will T-Bone."

"Me?" T-Bone choked on his coffee. He spun around on his stool and gaped at me.

"Well, you're the one with the experience here. At least you've helped cows give birth."

"I don't know . . ."

"Oh, please," begged Wynn; she liked the idea of having an authority consulting on her case.

T-Bone led us to his pickup truck, keeping a light grasp on Wynn's elbow as we crossed an icy patch. He helped her into the cab, tucked a blanket around her, and asked if she was warm enough. "Yes," said a surprised Wynn. Harvey, even in his heightened state of prenatal awareness, never offered a wrap.

I climbed in beside Wynn as T-Bone limped around the front of the truck to the driver's side. I noticed T-Bone didn't offer me so much as a dishcloth.

Lamaze classes were in the basement of the library. There were four couples, including the Winchesters. The instructor was a former obstetrics nurse. She was enthusiastic, supportive, perky. And skinny.

"She makes me want to throw up," Wynn said. "Harvey, of course, thinks she's wonderful."

We began with massage. "Remember coaches, a relaxed mother is a calmer mother," said the nurse. Enough said to the coaches, who jumped to stroking their partners. Apparently none of them wanted a hysterical fat woman on their hands.

I reached for Wynn. "No, let T-Bone," Wynn said, closing her eyes and laying flat on a mat, pillows propped under her knees and head.

I stared at T-Bone archly. He blushed and tentatively touched Wynn's arm.

"I won't break," Wynn said.

T-Bone stole a look at the couple on the next mat. He tried to imitate the father-to-be, working joint by joint, muscle by muscle, down to the toes. The father-to-be kept up a constant patter of soft, reassuring whispering.

I knew what Wynn was experiencing. T-Bone has gentle hands, soothing hands, hands accustomed to calming creatures. He doesn't grind or poke or punch, like some sadistic Swedish masseuse. Wynn relaxed. The tension poured out of her in buckets.

"What do I say to her?" T-Bone asked me. "Somehow, 'Cold enough for you lately?' doesn't cut it."

I shrugged. "Tell her what you know."

So T-Bone talked to Wynn of his farm and his cows, the way his land rolls from boundary to boundary and how he knows every bump. Soon, he told her, water will ripple through the hills. When the snow melted, his whole farm trickled with little streams, tiny waterfalls, microscopic rivers.

"I like to drive into the meadows and fields and see the earth waking up from winter. It makes me want to dance."

"Dance?" Wynn said, sleepily.

"Celebrate. Feel alive. Grow peaceful and whole, yet excited. As if the rivers are bubbling inside me. Life rushing to the surface in me."

"Yes," Wynn mur 'led, "like knitting squares for a baby's blanket."

I leaned back and closed my eyes, my only contact with the world T-Bone's mesmerizing voice. I thought of granny blanket squares, fitting together so perfectly, so prettily. There was Wynn, needles in hand. Look at her knit. She is incredible; she can't make a mistake even if she tries. Everyone wants an afghan by Wynn. People call her designs divine; surely that combination of hunter green and azure blue is inspired, they gush. "It's nothing," Wynn says biting the yarn with her teeth, "simply an old parka I found lying around the house and worked into the pattern of the afghan." Then she cavalierly tosses a scarf over her shoulder, lowers the hood on the hair dryer and returns to her knitting, looking for all the world like a grounded Amelia Earhart getting a perm.

Such daring, her fan club whispers.

I turn away. I could do that. I could be daring and courageous. I left the beauty shop, saddled up my cow and headed home to my studio . . .

"Maud. Maud! Will you wake up? We've got a situation here."

"What?" I rubbed my eyes then pried them open.

Wynn sat up holding her stomach. She looked as if she had just swallowed a half-baked doughnut.

"Is she sick?"

"We were starting the breathing exercises, whatever they are, and she grabbed her stomach."

"I'm conscious. You can talk to me."

"Well, what is it?" I said irritated. Cows in my dreams always made me grumpy.

"I think it's the baby."

"Now!" T-Bone gasped.

"Now!" I shouted.

We made the twenty-minute drive to the hospital in thirteen and a half minutes flat, hitting only one tree on a slippery curve west of town. As the orderlies wheeled Wynn's gurney away, she shouted, "Maud, call Harvey and tell him fuck the trees. Get his ass here now."

Harvey made it in time for the birth of his seven-pound, four-ounce girl with thick, black hair and fantastic eyelashes. At least, I think that was him, a blur flying through the waiting room, a chain saw extension cord trailing behind him.

T-Bone and I waited to see the baby. She didn't have any

neck, and she looked rather worn and wrinkled. She seemed to cry a lot. She needed a shampoo, blow-dry, and style. In short, she was beautiful.

T-Bone drove home slowly. The sun was just coming up. The weatherman on the radio forecasted a thaw. Just in time for Town Meeting Day. That'll be a picnic. At T-Bone's, we wearily milked the cows then crawled into bed with our clothes on. We held each other and waited for the same old dreams. But they didn't come. We slept in peace as did the tired Winchester family.

20

It Rained So Hard,
It Washed the Spots off the Holsteins

Rain. Nature carved the snowbanks with rain. Whittled out
monsters and animals and voluptuous women.

The frozen earth beneath the snow could not absorb the
slicing water. So the water skated. Down the mountain, through
the woods, across the pastures, over the roads. All the way to
Lake Champlain. Everywhere in Round Corners patches of
earth appeared. Dark spots dappled the snow, like the coat of a
holstein cow. People discovered they had yards and fences and
had forgotten to take in the rake last fall. Sheriff Odie Dorf-
mann's wife stared out her kitchen window at dozens of softballs,
a stadium of softballs.

It rained through the night and the dawn. The people of
Round Corners got up, looked out the window, and shrugged. It
didn't matter. Today was Town Meeting Day.

And the people of Round Corners loved Town Meeting.

By ten o'clock, the gymnasium of the Round Corners El-
ementary School was full of folks in galoshes and slickers. Rain
was, at that very moment, eating away at the white calling card
of the snowstorm seven days ago, the storm that kept Harvey
Winchester from attending his beloved Lamaze classes but
couldn't keep him away from his daughter's birthing room, the
storm that introduced T-Bone and me to the calm, watery world
of human babies.

The townspeople left cellars full of mud and drove roads
almost impassable from high water to get to Town Meeting.
"Didn't think I could get here," one man told another, "and don't
know if I'll get home."

In the back of the auditorium, the parents association was doing a brisk business in coffee and hot chocolate this cold, wet morning. Cake doughnuts were on sale for those who missed breakfast or needed something to stuff in the mouths of bored babies or loquacious orators. Proceeds were earmarked for new playground equipment, a contraption that looked part tree, part ship, and was called In the Swing of Things.

The purpose of Town Meeting was not only to put the town's business in order, but to restore and renew friendships frozen in place by the long winter. It was no fluke that Town Meeting was scheduled in March. News pushed forward, like a crocus in the snow, at Town Meeting. Friends, who had seen little of each other during the cold months, caught up on the events in their lives, the grandchildren who had been born, the sons and daughters who were away at college.

In one of the most independent forms of government, everyone was given the opportunity to have his or her say. Town Moderator Frank Snowden saw to it. He and his gavel kept the meeting running according to schedule and parliamentary procedure. Frank was known for his firmness, fairness, and a sense of humor capable of defusing hot situations. This meeting the people elected Frank to his tenth year as moderator. Ella, sitting in the front row, smiled: She'd told him he was a shoo-in.

Round Corners residents plowed through the agenda, loudly and clearly exercising their rights of free speech. The farmer with five hunting dogs objected to the proposed leash law. The woman sitting next to Reverend and Mrs. Swan set aside the dress she was hemming to ask several specific questions about the town budget. "Look at those numbers on page five, Herb. They just don't add up."

Herb, the town clerk, punched out a symphony on the calculator. "There's a mistake all right." The woman sighed in satisfaction. "Haven't you ever made a mistake, Louise?"

"Not that I remember," Louise said, "but if'n I did, I wouldn't advertise it in the town budget."

Round Corners people believed in stating their views simply

and bluntly. Opposition was not taken personally. "With all due respect to my neighbor," said one man, "he doesn't know what he's talking about."

I perched on a cold metal folding chair in the back of the gym beside Freda Lee. The chair on the other side was empty, saved for T-Bone. Every time the side door of the gymnasium swung open letting in latecomers and cold wind and rain, I strained to see if T-Bone was among them.

In the row in front of us were the Winchesters, holding hands and cradling sleeping Baby Winchester. Odie approached the podium, and Wynn turned around and winked at me. Behind the podium was a huge object draped in a white sheet.

"Too bad Thomas isn't here. He would have loved this," Freda whispered.

"Yes," I said.

The painting was as big as a queen-size bed. Thomas measured the space in the town hall, three times. "It's got to be this big," he said, showing me the numbers on a scrap of paper.

"That's too big," I said.

"No, it's not."

"I can't do it."

"Yes, you can."

Thomas really ought to be here with his bowls of soup ("Not cream of celery again") and his nagging about sleep and work and baths. No one, except T-Bone, had ever taken care of me like Thomas had. But Thomas was in Australia. According to his postcards, he was "chasing girls and building houses." The last card, sporting a koala clinging to a tree, said simply, "Well, what do you think?"

Not, did you finish it? Or, how's it going? The idealism of youth. The faith of Thomas.

Where was T-Bone? I squirmed in my seat.

All right, this is the absolutely first and last analysis of the painting. From here on out, I'm turning strictly stoic, cowboy tight-lipped, forget all this deep psychological symbolism shit. I'm not answering any questions after this. Picasso had his blue period. This is my talkative period. Catch it quick; it's going to last two minutes.

What do I think? I think somebody else did it.

My fingerprints are on it, but something there isn't mine, something there is beyond me.

I fought with that painting, waged war with it, struggled with it, pampered it, played with it, cared for it, cursed it, damned it, demanded things of it, pleaded with it, harangued it, ignored it, cried over it, warned it, screamed at it, listened to it, talked to it, supported it, protected it, defended it, watched over it, scowled at it, stuck my tongue out at it, snarled at it, threw paint at it, threw brushes at it, threw chairs at it, kicked it—and vowed to send it to the world's worst museum somewhere in the middle of the steamy jungle where the humidity would peel the paint right off the canvas.

If that's not love, what is?

When I was ten and the house attracted people like red sugar water does hummingbirds, I asked a sculptor passing through on his way to Montreal, "Have you ever tried to quit?"

He laughed, "I'd starve."

I frowned, and he pointed to his big, tangly beard.

He sculpted figures from rocks found in creeks and streams. The Rock Man waded in, barefoot, trousers rolled up to the calves, to collect the rocks. He said Vermont had cold creeks. He carved the rocks by chipping away at them with a dentist's drill. The drill worked like a tiny jackhammer.

The Rock Man said when he sculpted, rock dust flew up in his face, on his lips and beard. He liked to taste that salty stone spray, to lick his lips the way sailors do. Some stones, he said, were sweeter than others. The Rock Man carried around his own personal salt supply in his beard. If he were ever on a bus in the desert and it broke down and all the passengers had to walk to Vegas, he would make it, just by sucking on his facial hair.

When it was time for him to leave, to continue north, he thanked me for sharing my house with him and gave me a rock. It was a statue of a woman, and she was so at one with the stone that the Rock Man had hardly needed to carve her. Nature had designed with wind and water a gown in the stone, a perfect forehead, long thick hair. He simply added a nose here and a hand there.

"It is against the laws of nature," the Rock Man said, "to starve the soul."

Sounds profound. But then, those were the words of a guy who acquired his daily salt requirement from his beard.

At the podium, Odie blathered on about art and culture and mankind and civilization. Everyone wished Frank would use his gavel on Odie. Finally, Odie made his point, which wasn't much, and whisked off the sheet.

Silence. Not a baby cried. Not a chair creaked. Not a pin dropped (not even from Louise in the third row hemming her daughter's Easter dress).

Round Corners was caught unawares.

I held my breath. Wasn't someone going to say something? Whatever happened to "everyone's a critic"? There's never a critic around when you need one, I thought.

The painting, at first glance, appeared to be an overgrown greeting card. It began in the forefront with a herd of black-and-white cows, then swept up the hill to a tiny town, obviously Round Corners from the steeple on Our Lady of Perpetual Savings, to the windows of Snowden's General Store. Across the sky, the Vermont sky with stars hung low enough to touch, streaked a comet.

The people of Round Corners were disappointed. They had expected at least a few humans in the picture. Each secretly had hoped they would be chosen to be in the definitive statement of Round Corners. Slowly, my neighbors rose from their chairs, and as if the painting was reeling them in, they approached the front of the gym.

They crowded around it.

They began to whisper, talk, laugh. As their excitement grew, so did their voices.

"Look at the cows."

"Look at the spots on the cows."

"They're full of little pictures. Little pictures inside the big picture."

"There's Wynn setting someone's hair."

"Where?"

"There. The second cow from the left."

"I can't see. Do I have blonde hair?"

"And there's Frank waiting on a child at the candy counter."

"That looks like my Tommy."

"No, it doesn't, that's my little Alphonse. See the hole in his shoe?"

"My Tommy has holes in his shoes, too."

"And there's a softball game."

"I bet I'm the one at bat. Am I the one at bat?"

"No, Sheriff."

"That's the Round Corners Restaurant . . ."

"Hey, Bartholomew, it's a wonder you didn't break the canvas."

"I thought the saying was 'break the camera,' Amos."

"And there's a picture of the church . . ."

"You look positively zealous, Samuel dear."

"Do you think so?"

"Why there must be dozens of little pictures hidden in that herd of cows."

"Isn't that cute!"

George couldn't have said it better. I rose slowly from my folding chair, flipped up the hood of my raincoat, and went looking for T-Bone.

One of T-Bone's cows died the day of Town Meeting.

The veterinarian diagnosed it as milk fever, caused by shortages of or an imbalance of calcium or phosphorus. Cows that are going to calve or that have calved are particularly susceptible to the disease. A developing calf, like a human baby, places a heavy demand on the nutrients eaten by the mother. It is important that the farmer check the pregnant cow's ration for minerals and vitamins. One of the first symptoms of milk fever is paralysis of the rear legs. The cow goes down and cannot get up again. In other words, the cow can't dance anymore.

"Milk fever," the vet said, after examining the cow. "No doubt about it."

I found T-Bone after the vet had gone, cradling the head of the dead cow. "No doubt about it," he said. "The cow died from lack of a radio."

"Don't be ridiculous," I said.

"Cows need music, too."

"This is a farm, not Radio City Music Hall. Animals are born here, and they die here all the time. This is a life cycle factory."

"It's my fault," he said. "Where was I when she needed me? Why didn't I notice before it got this far?" I patted T-Bone's arm, worried. He usually took such events—the life-and-death continuum of the farm—with equanimity. He worried about everything and anything but the way he did his job. That was one area T-Bone was always sure of. Until now.

He stood abruptly. "I've got to bury her."

"Now? In the rain?"

"You wait here," he told the dead cow.

If he had been thinking straight, T-Bone simply would have taken the cow to a plant that disposes of large animals. He would have realized that was the most economical, the most efficient, the most sensible plan. He would have known better than to try to bury a half-ton cow on his frozen farm. Instead, the unthinking T-Bone chose for the grave a spot on top of the hill behind the barn. "Whenever possible, humans are buried on high ground," T-Bone said, half limping, half pacing back and forth, stopping every third lap to again survey the cemetery plot on the hill.

"Please let me fix you a warm cup of hot chocolate," I said.

"High places are closer to God," T-Bone said. "Not to mention, how difficult it is to rest in peace in a swamp."

"A Rolling Rock," I said. "Let me get a couple of beers, and we'll sit down and talk about the situation."

"I read in the newspaper they're gonna bury people in space.

Shoot their ashes into the galaxy. From dust to cosmic dust."
T-Bone didn't approve of dumping stuff in space. He had diffi-
culty acknowledging that what goes up does not always come
down and worried that someday people would be dropping like
snowflakes from the sky.

"No, the hill will be just fine," he said, then turned and
marched out into the rain.

I ran after him. "Wait. Please T-Bone. This is crazy."

"No," T-Bone gave me a salute. "This is mud season." Then
grabbing a shovel leaning against the barn, he strode up the hill.

T-Bone attacked the frozen ground with the shovel, the rain
running down his neck, his booted feet sliding in the thin layer of
mud the rain had defrosted. He worked until he was sweating
under his wet clothes, with little result. I stood beside him, the
rain running down my nose.

"What I need," he shouted, "is a backhoe or a tractor. It *is* a
big cow."

He ran slipping and sliding down the hill, hopped aboard the
tractor, and revved it to life. He gunned the tractor up the hill.
The tractor's big tires gripped the incline and pulled; they spun
and slipped. T-Bone gritted his teeth, squinted his eyes against
the downpour, and shifted into low gear, climbing gear, goat
gear. It did not occur to him he had nothing attached to the
tractor with which to dig a hole, neither a small nor a large hole.
And he would need a monstrous hole.

He hurdled the tractor at the hill again. It lunged. The wheels
grabbed for ground but grasped air. There was no ground—
the entire hill was collapsing under nature's watery knife. I
screamed, "Jump!" T-Bone felt the tractor begin to tip. He
leaped. One after another, they tumbled down the hill, like
children in a nursery rhyme. T-Bone came to a stop, sprawled
face in the mud, the jackhammer rain beating his back.

I scrambled down the hill, sliding to his side as if it were home
plate. "T-Bone," I yelled over the deluge. "Are you hurt?" I
tugged at his arm, trying to help him to his feet. He jerked away.
I sighed.

We struggled to our feet. "Mind if I use your van?" he asked, heading around the barn.

"No!"

"You're right. It barely runs on flat terrain."

"Please give this up," I begged. "I'll bury the cow."

T-Bone stopped and turned to me. "You will?"

I nodded.

"Promise?"

"Sure. Why don't you go in the house and rest for a while? I bet you're tired."

T-Bone rubbed his eye with a muddy hand. "A nap would be nice."

Slowly, I took his arm and guided him toward the house. "You'll feel like a different man after a nap."

T-Bone leaned against me. "You know, Maud, I worry about you."

"I know."

"I've always tried to take care of you."

"And you've done a good job, too."

"I have?"

I settled T-Bone on the sofa in the office with an afghan on his legs and Cat on his chest. He was already asleep by the time I called the vet and made arrangements for someone to pick up the cow tomorrow. I glanced at my watch. Four o'clock. My shift at the Round Corners Restaurant had started at three.

Every year Town Meeting adjourned to the Round Corners Restaurant. People, with the taste of power in their mouths, couldn't just go home to grilled cheese and chips. Governing, tossing power around like a beach ball, built up an appetite. They were loud and laughing as they placed their orders. Freda Lee says this is what happens when you give people the chance to talk: You can't shut them up. If nothing else, Town Meeting was therapeutic. People let off steam, complained, griped, told off City Hall, and were happy for the next twelve months.

The rain chased away the skiers, which meant the locals had the restaurant to themselves, and they took up every table and booth. Freda and I kept the coffee flowing. The customers ordered sandwiches mostly: Odie, Amos, and Bartholomew, cheeseburger deluxes; Ella Snowden, Reverend Swan, and Mrs. Swan, BLT on toast; Frank Snowden and Harvey Winchester, turkey club. Wynn Winchester said she'd have a salad, thank you, that's all.

The kid in the kitchen complained.

"What are you grinning about?" I said to Freda.

She blushed.

Lewis Lee had dropped in earlier, out of the blue, just back from hauling a load of logs, and said he would pick her up after work.

"I've got my car," Freda said.

"I don't want you driving that little thing on these roads," Lewis Lee said. "I'll wait for you out back, like I used to do."

Freda nodded shyly.

Freda began working at the Round Corners Restaurant twenty-five years ago when she was a junior in high school. She was in love with Lewis Lee even back then. She worked two nights during the week and Friday night on the weekend. She missed most football games. She always told Lewis to go to the postgame party without her. Lewis always waited.

On the nights she knew Lewis was waiting for her behind the restaurant in his old blue Ford, she flew through closing: vacuuming, sweeping, filling the sugar containers. She did everything the older waitresses told her to do in half the time. Then, when they were satisfied and said, go on, take off, she dashed into the rest room, brushed her teeth, wiggled out of the polyester uniform and into blue jeans, combed her hair, and sprayed her arms and neck with perfume, praying it covered the smell of grease, sweat, and hamburger.

Lewis's friends couldn't understand why he put up with all the logistical problems of dating a working girl like Freda. Don't you ever get tired of it? they asked. Tired of waiting out behind the Round Corners Restaurant? Tired of arriving late at all the parties? Lewis Lee, the latest issue of a long line of stoic New

Englanders, merely shrugged. He couldn't explain it. He just knew he'd rather be waiting for Freda than partying with any other girl.

Freda patted her hair. Lewis had liked the new hairstyle, once it grew out a little. He said she looked real dangerous. "Reminds me of one of those women on afternoon television."

Freda smiled at the memory.

"I wonder if I've still got that bottle of perfume in my purse."
Ding, ding, ding.

"Some day," Freda said, straightening her apron, "I'm going to ram that bell . . ."

The cook was saved a clapper in the Adam's apple by the jangle of another bell, the one over the door to the Round Corners Restaurant.

"You've got to stop him!" cried the bell ringer. "Someone's got to stop him!"

The woman, dripping in the doorway of the Round Corners Restaurant, wore no coat. She was soaked and hysterical. I hardly recognized the woman shivering and screaming as the president of the parents association. Last time I saw her she was the picture of control, coolly arranging doughnuts and Danish pastries on a big tray in the school gymnasium.

"Stop who?" said Odie, jumping to his feet. A picture of readiness. Exhibiting the quick reflexes of a lawman or a pitcher of the Round Corners Royals.

"That Mr. T-Bone. He's about to destroy the painting."

"Oh, no," I gasped, shoving a salad in Freda's hand and hurdling over the counter.

Freda slid the salad on a nearby table and followed me as did everyone else in the restaurant. The restaurant emptied like an overturned hourglass. People streamed into the darkening evening, never-minding the rain, forgetting coats. Somewhere a bell dinged wildly.

President Hysterical caught up with me. "I was just washing out the coffeepots, they hold thirty cups, you know, when he came in, carrying a chain saw. He looked like one of those mass murderers in the movies, wild eyes, muddy clothes, ghastly face, carrying a chain saw. Don't kill me, I pleaded . . ."

The ground was a skating rink of mud. I ran faster, cutting through backyards, slipping in the field of softballs at Odie's house. I took the corner at Wynn's shop too close and crashed into a bush. Behind me was a trail of soaked, mud-covered, slipping and sliding, cursing townspeople. Occasionally, one fell and the air turned blue with commentary. "Damn, Odie, what'd you do—booby-trap your yard with softballs? Catch many criminals this way?"

We heard the buzz of the chain saw before we reached the gymnasium double doors. It was a lonely sound in the dark, forlorn as a saxophone, wild as a songbird. It came out of the rain to terrify us and tease us and douse us with despair. I ran harder, splashing across the street, hoping it wasn't too late.

We poured into the gymnasium, wet and gasping, and skidded promptly to a halt.

T-Bone froze at the sound of the gymnasium doors crashing against the wall. He held the blade of the saw at the top of the painting. I squeezed my eyes shut, waiting to hear the keening, ear-splitting scream of the saw as it slowly cut the picture in half. I held my breath, listening for the moment when the chain saw chewed through canvas, frame, wall; through artery, muscle, bone; through grass, dirt, earthworm; through gas, light, space dust.

T-Bone stepped back. He shut off the motor. Silence rang in our ears. The chain saw fell from his hands. It crashed to the gym floor, and T-Bone jerked, as if being frightened awake. He stared at the painting, lifted a hand to it, a beseeching hand, a gentle hand, but did not touch it. He turned and looked at me.

Finally, I moved. Water squished out of my wet, rubber-soled shoes. Slowly I approached T-Bone across the gym floor. T-Bone never took his eyes off me. My uniform clung to my body; my hair curled around my face. My heart roared in my ears. I came to a halt before him; we studied each other.

"I've always loved you, y'know," he whispered. After a long

moment, I lifted a hand and smoothed his ruffled hair. He groaned, grabbed my hand, and held it against his cheek.

"Is that what stopped you?" I asked.

T-Bone turned to study the painting. He shook his head. "Suddenly, I realized, it's just a painting."

"Yeah, I know."

"It's not the savior of Round Corners, and it's not a rival for your affections. It's simply paint and canvas. The *real* painting of Round Corners is inside you. It gives you a glow. I saw that glow in a little girl with long legs and a face full of hair, and I remember thinking, even though I was only seventeen: That glow could warm me forever. I found that glow when I danced and when I was near you."

T-Bone blushed. It was quite a speech for him. He looked at his feet, pulled back his shoulders, and said in a voice I hadn't heard in a long time, the old T-Bone, "I see my cows, but I don't see me."

"I never could draw you."

"You've made a million sketches of me."

"But none were ever right. I try again and again, and they're never you."

"Maybe I'm elusive, the man of contradictions, the dairy farmer who can't keep his cows alive, the clumsy tap dancer."

"Or maybe you just mean too much to me," I said. "Maybe there is no canvas big enough in my heart to contain you." T-Bone turned and stared at me. I smiled and held out my hand. "Dance with me, T-Bone."

T-Bone's eyebrows jerked in surprise, and he took a step back in fear. I took a step forward. He retreated again. I advanced with a giant step, slapped my hand on his shoulder, and looked pointedly at his left hand. Awkwardly, he folded my hand in his. We shuffled slowly, at first. He leaned on me a little, and I edged closer to him. I dropped my head on his shoulder, and I felt his arm circle my waist. Slowly we circled the gymnasium.

Like the king and queen at the homecoming dance, like the bride and groom at the wedding, we moved in a world of our

own until one by one the others joined us. Frank was the first to
whisk Ella out onto the floor. The Reverend and Mrs. Swan
waltzed past next. Odie offered his arm to Louise the sewing
grandmother. The Winchesters danced with Baby Winchester
sandwiched between them, asleep in a Snugli strapped to
Harvey's chest.

Someone flipped on a radio, and soon everyone was whirling
and twirling, slapping their muddy feet on the polished gymna-
sium floor. They laughed and spun each other around, they do-
si-doed, they tangoed. They did the electric slide and slipped into
each other.

As night fell, the townspeople drifted home, humming in the
rain. They felt almost light-headed. They told themselves it was
because the painting was safe. But if that was true, they won-
dered, why did they have other things on their minds?

That night in bed Wynn Winchester whispered to her hus-
band, while he held her in his arms, "I think the baby's new
sweater ought to be in lavender, don't you think?" Odie Dorf-
mann told his wife, while he crawled into his baseball pajamas,
that he had "an idea for a series of birdhouses—homes of the
presidents." Reverend Swan prayed for Round Corners that
night, and when he was finished, he made the sign of the cross,
just the way his Catholic mother had taught him. Ella Snowden
began a new poem about Round Corners that night; she fell
asleep at the kitchen table, and early in the morning Frank gently
removed the pen from her fingers, lifted her into his arms, and
put her to bed.

I took T-Bone home, stood him in a hot shower, and then
joined him. I tucked him in bed and snuggled in beside him. The
rain stopped. I saw a star through the window. And suddenly, I
felt light, as if I were stardust, too, and shining through the
window of someone else in some other world.

21

Say Good-Bye, George

I thump George's headstone, not too hard, really more out of habit.

George, it has occurred to me that our conversations are fairly one-sided. I don't think I want to talk to you anymore. You always did expect too much. This is a perfect example. You expect me to still keep talking to you after you're dead. Expectations, I have discovered, will kill you. That may not be something you have to worry about, but as for me . . .

The sun is warm on my face. The day is tempting with a taste of summer, a hot hors d'oeuvre offered in May. It's not a bad day at all to sit in a graveyard under the budding trees. I can lean back against George's tombstone, rest my head, and just dream.

At home, T-Bone is cooking dinner. He's making pizza, from scratch, probably whistling. He gets into anything involving dough. Jazz is sneaking out of the radio, loud enough to blow your eardrums; when I pull into the drive, I'll see him through the window, diving for the radio knob, and giving it a quick spin to Catfish Joe's show. He says he's beginning to like country and western. Sure.

T-Bone's still a worrier. He worries about my eating habits, the price of milk, if he's feeding the birds too much and ruining them for life in the "real natural world."

He worries about everything. But my painting.

The Round Corners painting hangs in the Town Hall. Everyone who enters the Town Hall to pay a traffic ticket or complain about a fuel bill takes it upon himself to straighten the picture. The cows are always cockeyed.

I enter my studio every day. And sometimes I even paint something other than cows.

What do you mean not often, *George? I don't know why I even talk to you when you're like this, when you're in your know-it-all mood. What about the house? How did we get on the house? I think it looks great. White is not nice. White is for sissies, George. And I'd like to know what you know about houses and art. For your information,* House Beautiful *is doing a story on my house.*

Not really. But as I said, having the last word is important sometimes.

About the Author

Sherry Roberts is the coauthor of *Greensboro: A New American Metropolis.* Her nonfiction work—features and essays—appears in *USA Today,* the *New York Times Book Review, Compute, Christian Science Monitor, Business North Carolina, Business Life, The State,* and *Carolina Piedmont.* She has had short stories published in *The Crucible, The Inkling,* and *Golden Triad* as well as the *1985 O. Henry Festival Stories,* the *1993 O. Henry Festival Stories,* and newspaper syndications. Ms. Roberts spent seven years in Vermont, where it is possible to see both the art in a cow and the cow dung in art.

Quality Books from Papier-Mache Press

At Papier-Mache Press our goal is to produce attractive, accessible books that deal with contemporary personal, social, and political issues. Our titles have found an enthusiastic audience in general interest, women's, new age, and religious bookstores, as well as gift stores, mail order catalogs, and libraries. Many have also been used by teachers for women's studies, creative writing, and gerontology classes, and by therapists and family counselors to help clients explore personal issues such as aging and relationships.

   If you are interested in finding out more about our other titles, ask your local bookstores which Papier-Mache items they carry. Or, if you would like to receive a complete catalog of books, posters, and shirts from Papier-Mache Press, please send a self-addressed stamped envelope to:

Papier-Mache Press
135 Aviation Way, #14
Watsonville, CA 95076